AMERICAN POLITICAL, ECONOMIC,

# DOLLAR DEPRECIATION:
# ECONOMIC EFFECTS
# AND POLICY RESPONSE

# AMERICAN POLITICAL, ECONOMIC, AND SECURITY ISSUES

Additional books in this series can be found on Nova's website
under the Series tab.

Additional E-books in this series can be found on Nova's website
under the E-books tab.

AMERICAN POLITICAL, ECONOMIC, AND SECURITY ISSUES

# DOLLAR DEPRECIATION: ECONOMIC EFFECTS AND POLICY RESPONSE

## LACHLAN S. ROY
### EDITOR

**Nova Science Publishers, Inc.**
*New York*

For permission to use material from this book please contact us:
Telephone 631-231-7269; Fax 631-231-8175
Web Site: http://www.novapublishers.com

## NOTICE TO THE READER

The Publisher has taken reasonable care in the preparation of this book, but makes no expressed or implied warranty of any kind and assumes no responsibility for any errors or omissions. No liability is assumed for incidental or consequential damages in connection with or arising out of information contained in this book. The Publisher shall not be liable for any special, consequential, or exemplary damages resulting, in whole or in part, from the readers' use of, or reliance upon, this material. Any parts of this book based on government reports are so indicated and copyright is claimed for those parts to the extent applicable to compilations of such works.

Independent verification should be sought for any data, advice or recommendations contained in this book. In addition, no responsibility is assumed by the publisher for any injury and/or damage to persons or property arising from any methods, products, instructions, ideas or otherwise contained in this publication.

This publication is designed to provide accurate and authoritative information with regard to the subject matter covered herein. It is sold with the clear understanding that the Publisher is not engaged in rendering legal or any other professional services. If legal or any other expert assistance is required, the services of a competent person should be sought. FROM A DECLARATION OF PARTICIPANTS JOINTLY ADOPTED BY A COMMITTEE OF THE AMERICAN BAR ASSOCIATION AND A COMMITTEE OF PUBLISHERS.

Additional color graphics may be available in the e-book version of this book.

## Library of Congress Cataloging-in-Publication Data

Dollar depreciation : economic effects and policy response / editor, Lachlan S. Roy.
    p. cm.
  Includes index.
  ISBN 978-1-61470-692-2 (softcover)
  1. Dollar, American. 2. Foreign exchange rates--United States. 3. Devaluation of currency--United States. 4. United States--Foreign economic relations. I. Roy, Lachlan S.
  HG540.D647 2011
  332.4'1420973--dc23
                        2011024890

*Published by Nova Science Publishers, Inc. † New York*

# CONTENTS

# PREFACE

A trend depreciation of the dollar since 2002 raises concern among some in Congress and the public that the dollar's decline is a symptom of broader economic problems, such as a weak economic recovery, rising public debt, and a diminished standing in the global economy. However, a failing currency is not always a problem, but possibly an element of economic adjustments that are, on balance, beneficial to the economy. This book examines the economic context in which to view the dollar's recent and prospective movement, and analyzes the evolution of the exchange rate since its peak in 2002. It also discusses several factors that are likely to influence the dollar's medium-term path, what effects a depreciating dollar could have on the economy, and how alternative policy measures that could be taken by the Federal Reserve and the Treasury might influence the dollar's path.

Chapter 1- A trend depreciation of the dollar since 2002 raises concern among some in Congress and the public that the dollar's decline is a symptom of broader economic problems, such as a weak economic recovery, rising public debt, and a diminished standing in the global economy. However, a falling currency is not always a problem, but possibly an element of economic adjustments that are, on balance, beneficial to the economy.

Chapter 2- The dollar's value in international exchange has been falling since early 2002. Over this five year span, the currency, on a real trade weighted basis, is down about 25%. For most of this time the dollar's fall was moderately paced at about 2.0% to 5.0% annually. Recently, however, the slide has accelerated, falling about 9% between January and December of 2007. An acceleration of the depreciation brings the periodic concern of an impending dollar crisis to the fore. There is no precise demarcation of when a falling dollar moves from being an orderly decline to being a crisis. Most likely it would be a situation where the dollar falls, perhaps 15% to 20% annually for several years, and sends a significant negative shock to the U.S. and the global economies. A crisis may not be an inevitable outcome, but one that likely presents considerable risk to the economy.

Chapter 3- Globally, central bank holdings of reserve currency assets have risen sharply in recent years. These "official holdings" have nearly tripled since 1999 to reach $5 trillion by the end of 2006. Nearly $3 trillion has been amassed by developing Asia and Japan. China, in particular, now has official reserves that exceed $1 trillion. In addition, the oil-exporting countries have increased their official reserves by about $700 billion. The dollar's status as the dominant international currency has meant that as much 70% of this large accumulation of official reserves are of some form of dollar asset.

Chapter 4- Rapid changes in the price of oil and the impact of such price changes on economies around the globe have attracted considerable attention. In mid-2008 as the price of oil rose to unprecedented heights and then dropped sharply, the international exchange value of the dollar fell and then rose relative to a broad basket of currencies. For some, these two events seem to indicate a cause and effect relationship between changes in the price of oil and changes in the value of the dollar. Despite common perceptions that there is a direct cause and effect relationship between changes in the international exchange value of the dollar and the price of oil, an analysis of data during recent periods indicates that changes in the price of oil are driven by changes in the demand for oil that is different from the supply of oil, rather than changes in the value of the dollar. The rapid increase in oil prices in early 2011 reflects rising demand for oil and other commodities and uncertainty in global markets keyed to political turmoil in North Africa and the Middle East.

In: Dollar Depreciation  
Editor: Lachlan S. Roy

ISBN: 978-1-61470-692-2  
© 2011 Nova Science Publishers, Inc.

*Chapter 1*

# THE DEPRECIATING DOLLAR: ECONOMIC EFFECTS AND POLICY RESPONSE[*]

## *Craig K. Elwell*

## SUMMARY

A trend depreciation of the dollar since 2002 raises concern among some in Congress and the public that the dollar's decline is a symptom of broader economic problems, such as a weak economic recovery, rising public debt, and a diminished standing in the global economy. However, a falling currency is not always a problem, but possibly an element of economic adjustments that are, on balance, beneficial to the economy.

A depreciating currency could affect several aspects of U.S. economic performance. Possible effects include increased net exports, decreased international purchasing power, rising commodity prices, and upward pressure on interest rates; if the trend is sustained, reduction of external debt, possible undermining of the dollar's reserve currency status, and an elevated risk of a dollar crisis.

The exchange rate is not a variable that is easily addressed by changes in legislative policy. Nevertheless, although usually not the primary target, the dollar's international value can be affected by decisions made on policy issues facing the 112th Congress, including decisions related to generating jobs, raising the debt limit, reducing the budget deficit, and stabilizing the growth of the federal government's

---

[*] This is an edited, reformatted and augmented version of a Congressional Research Service publication, CRS Report for Congress RL34582, from www.crs.gov, dated April 15, 2011.

long-term debt. Also monetary policy actions by the Federal Reserve, over which Congress has oversight responsibilities, can affect the dollar.

The exchange rate of the dollar is largely determined by the market—the supply and demand for dollars in global foreign exchange markets. In most circumstances, however, international asset-market transactions will tend to be dominant, with the size and strength of inflows and outflows of capital ultimately determining whether the exchange rate appreciates or depreciates.

A variety of factors can influence the size and direction of cross-border asset flows. Of principal importance are the likely rate of return on the asset, investor expectations about a currency's future path, the size and liquidity of the country's asset markets, the need for currency diversification in international investors' portfolios, changes in the official holdings of foreign exchange reserves by central banks, and the need for and location of investment safe havens. All of these factors could themselves be influenced by economic policy choices.

To give Congress the economic context in which to view the dollar's recent and prospective movement, this report analyzes the evolution of the exchange rate since its peak in 2002. It examines several factors that are likely to influence the dollar's medium-term path, what effects a depreciating dollar could have on the economy, and how alternative policy measures that could be taken by the Federal Reserve, the Treasury, and the 112th Congress might influence the dollar's path.

## INTRODUCTION

From a peak in early 2002 to mid-2008, the (inflation adjusted) trade-weighted dollar exchange rate, for the most part, steadily depreciated, falling a total of about 26% (see Figure 1). The dollar's fall over this six-year period was moderately paced at about 3% to 4% annually. For the next nine months, as the wider economy was reeling from the effects of the financial crisis and recession, the dollar sharply appreciated, increasing more than 11% on a trade-weighted basis.[1] For reasons that will be discussed later in the report, this appreciation was a market response to the great uncertainty associated with those economic troubles. As economic conditions began to stabilize in mid-2009, the dollar began to depreciate again and has fallen about 10% through the end of 2010.

The dollar's fall from 2002 through early 2008 as well as the recent depreciation has not been uniform against individual currencies, however. For example, in the earlier period, it fell 45% against the euro, 24% against the yen, 18% against the yuan, and 17% against the Mexican peso. In the period since the trough of the business cycle in mid-2009, the dollar fell 13% against the euro, 11% against the yen, less than 3% against the yuan (all of which occurred recently), and 8% against the peso.

These differing amounts of depreciation are partly a reflection of the countries' willingness to let their currencies fluctuate against the dollar. The euro is free floating, the yen has been moderately managed (mostly before 2005 but more deliberately since September 2010), and the yuan is actively managed (its value rigidly fixed to the dollar before 2005 and from mid-2008 until mid-2010; since then allowed to rise moderately against the dollar).[2] But the pattern also reflects significant structural asymmetries in flows of global assets and global goods, as well as differences in business cycles, inflation rates, shocks affecting the different economies, and an unwinding of imbalances that were present in 2002.[3]

The weakening of the dollar raises concern in Congress and among the public that the dollar's decline is a symptom of broader economic problems, such as a weak economic recovery, rising public debt, and a diminished standing in the global economy. Have recent policy actions such as quantitative easing by the Federal Reserve (Fed) and fiscal stimulus passed by the 111th Congress had an effect on the dollar? How might failure by the 112th Congress to raise the federal debt ceiling or address the country's long-term government debt problem affect the exchange rate? Is there a positive side to dollar depreciation?

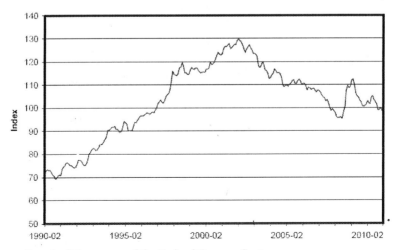

Source: Board of Governors of the Federal Reserve System.

Figure 1. Trade-Weighted Exchange Rate of Dollar.

Economic theory suggests that the dollar's path can be influenced by a variety of factors that could confer to the United States both benefits and costs, and in some circumstances a depreciating currency can be, on balance, beneficial. This report examines the several factors that are likely to influence the dollar's medium-term path; why further depreciation could occur; what effects a depreciating dollar could have on the economy, including the pace of economic recovery; and how alternative policy measures might influence the dollar's path.

## BROAD ECONOMIC FORCES THAT AFFECT THE DOLLAR

Since the break-up of the Bretton Woods international monetary system in 1973, the exchange rate of the dollar has been largely determined by the market—the supply and demand for dollars in global foreign exchange markets. Dollars are demanded by foreigners to buy dollar denominated goods and assets. (Assets include bank accounts, stocks, bonds, and real property.) Dollars are supplied to the foreign exchange markets by Americans exchanging them for foreign currencies typically needed to buy foreign goods and assets.

Since the mid-1990s, the United States has had a growing trade deficit in goods transactions, generating a net increase in the supply of dollars on the foreign exchange markets, thereby exerting downward pressure on the dollar's exchange rate. At the same time, the United States has had an equal-sized surplus in asset transactions, reflecting a net increase in the demand for dollars on the foreign exchange market, thereby exerting upward pressure on the dollar's exchange rate. [4]

In most circumstances, however, there is a strong expectation that asset-market transactions will tend to be dominant and ultimately dictate the exchange rate's direction of movement. This dominance is the result of gross asset-market transactions occurring on a scale and at a speed that greatly exceeds what occurs with goods-market transactions. Electronic exchange makes most asset transfers nearly instantaneous and, in most years, U.S.-international asset transactions were two to three times as large as what would be needed to simply finance that year's trade deficit.

In 2007, near the peak of the last economic expansion, the U.S. capital account recorded $1.5 trillion in purchases of foreign assets by U.S. residents (representing a capital outflow) and $2.1 trillion in purchases of U.S. assets by foreign residents (representing a capital inflow). So while the United States could have financed the $702 billion trade deficit in goods and services in 2007 simply by a $702 billion sale of assets to foreigners, U.S. and foreign investors engaged in a much larger volume of pure asset trading.[5]

# DETERMINANTS OF THE SIZE AND DIRECTION OF CROSS-BORDER ASSET FLOWS

Economic theory suggests that several economic factors could influence the direction of cross-border asset flows.

## Interest Rate Differentials between the United States and Other Economies

The demand for assets (e.g., bank accounts, stocks, bonds, and real property) by foreigners will be strongly influenced by the *expected rate of return* on those assets. Therefore, differences in the level of interest rates between economies are, other things equal, likely to stimulate international capital flows from countries with relatively low interest rates to countries with relatively high interest rates, as investors seek the highest rate of return for any given level of risk. When inflation rates among economies are similar, the average level of nominal interest rates can be used as a fairly reliable first approximation of the rate of return on an asset in a particular currency.

Rates of return on dollar assets can be influenced by the general performance of the economy as gauged by its ability to sustain a high rate of economic growth and a low rate of inflation. Another potential influence on expected rate of return is the Fed's conduct of monetary policy as it periodically moves interest rates up or down to stabilize the economy. In addition, whether the United States business cycle is synchronous or asynchronous with that of other economies will influence the relative level of interest rates between it and other economies. In general, these relatively short-term interest rate fluctuations will tend to either attract or deter foreign capital flows, particularly in relatively liquid assets.

The rate of return advantage in the U.S. economy may be greater than the spread between market interest rates would suggest, however. A study by the International Monetary Fund (IMF) that focused on return to debt and equity capital for publicly traded companies in the large industrial economies and the developing economies for the decade 1994-2003 found the rate of return in the United States to have been about 8.6% as compared with a G-7[6] average of about 2.4% and an emerging market average of about *minus* 4.7%.[7]

Currently, the combination of substantial economic slack and highly stimulative monetary policy in the United States and other advanced economies has pushed down short-term and long-term interest rates to historically low levels and left virtually no sizable interest rate advantage of dollar assets over assets in the currencies of other G-7 economies. For example, the yields on 10- year government bonds in Germany, Canada, the United Kingdom, and the United States during 2010 have been within a narrow band of 3.0% to 3.5%. Japan, however, has been an outlier among advanced economies, with the yield on 10-year government bonds hovering slightly above 1% over this period. In contrast, many emerging economies are showing much stronger economic performance and asset yields are likely to be substantially above those in the United States and other advanced economies, which could entice many investors to move capital from the advanced economies to the emerging economies. This would exert downward pressure on the currencies of the advanced economies, including the dollar.

## Investors' Expectations About the Future Path of the Dollar

Whether a currency's exchange rate will rise or fall in the future can figure prominently in some investors' calculation of what will actually be earned from an investment denominated in another currency. If, for example, the dollar depreciated on average 4% annually for the next several years, then the 2% to 4% average nominal interest rates currently attached to low-risk medium to long-term U.S. securities would offer the foreign investor an expected return of approximately zero or less. (If the expected currency depreciation were greater, the investor would expect to incur a capital loss.) In general, expected dollar depreciation lowers the expected return and reduces the attractiveness of dollar assets to the foreign investor. On the other hand, if the exchange rate is expected to appreciate, the expected gain would be greater than the nominal interest rate attached to the security, making that asset more attractive. Investor expectations will, therefore, tend to act as an accelerant, adding momentum to the exchange rates movement, whether up or down. At the extremes this could be destabilizing, generating sizable overvaluations or under-valuations of a currency.

The dollar's long and generally orderly depreciation between 2002 and 2008 suggests investor expectations about the currency's path did not act as a destabilizing factor. Nevertheless, the prospect of a secular depreciation likely reduced the attractiveness of dollar denominated assets to foreign investors at that time, and if the current depreciation of the dollar is seen as a resumption of that secular depreciation the attractiveness of dollar assets could also continue to be eroded.

## Investors Diversifying Their Portfolio of Assets

For any given interest rate differential and level of the exchange rate, international investors are likely to have a desired balance of assets in their portfolios, allocated not only among types of assets but also by the currency the assets are denominated in. As the stocks they hold of particular assets change over time, investors may see the need to rebalance their portfolios, shifting asset flows away from or toward assets denominated in a particular currency.

Such rebalancing can cause exchange rates for the denominating currency to increase or decrease as well.[8] For example, even if dollar assets offer a relatively high return, at some point foreign investors, considering both risk and reward, could decide that their portfolio's share of dollar-denominated assets is large enough. To mitigate exposure to currency risk in their portfolios, investors could slow or halt their purchase of dollar assets and increase their holdings of non-dollar assets. Such a diversification, other things equal, would tend to depreciate the dollar.

How much pure diversification from dollar assets is likely to happen over the near-term is difficult to determine. Nevertheless, with nearly $10 trillion in U.S. securities estimated to be in foreign investor portfolios, diversification toward other currencies could arguably be a factor of growing importance.[9] However, over the near-term, the general economic fragility of other advanced economies could mean there will be a lack of strong alternatives to dollar assets, tending to limit international investors' willingness to diversify into assets denominated in other currencies. On the other hand, the recent strong growth of many emerging economies could make them an increasingly attractive alternative destination for international capital flows.

## Other Factors that Influence the International Demand for Dollar Assets

Beyond the standard determinants of risk and reward that are likely to have a strong near-term influence on the relative attractiveness of dollar-denominated assets, the United States has some added advantages that are thought to generate a sustained underlying demand for dollar assets.

### *The Size and Liquidity of U.S. Asset Markets*

Large asset markets, such as those in the United States, offer a great variety of asset types and a high degree of liquidity. This means that these asset markets are able to handle large inflows and outflows of funds with only a small impact on the price of the asset. Recent IMF estimates of the relative size of the asset markets in the advanced economies show that in 2009 the U.S. bond market had a total value of nearly $32 trillion (with government bonds accounting for about $9.5 trillion of that), whereas the United Kingdom, Germany, and Japan had much smaller bond markets with a total value of about $4.7 trillion, $5.7 trillion, and $12 trillion, respectively. In addition, the U.S. stock market has an estimated capitalized value of nearly $15 trillion, whereas the United Kingdom, Germany, and Japan's equity markets were estimated to have capitalized values of about $2.8 trillion, $1.3 trillion, and $3.4 trillion, respectively.[10]

A good example of a large highly liquid asset market is that for U.S. Treasury securities, which has been particularly attractive to foreign investors in recent years. Federal Reserve data show that for the week ending February 23, 2011, the U.S. government securities markets had a daily turnover of about $680 billion. Additional evidence of the high liquidity of U.S. government securities market is its typically small bid-ask spreads. On relatively short-term Treasury securities, the spread is usually a few tenths of a cent per $100 dollar face value of the security.[11]

In recent years, the high liquidity of dollar assets has been an attractive feature for foreign central banks, which have been rapidly increasing their holdings of foreign exchange reserves, a substantial portion of which are thought to be dollar assets. The same is true for petroleum exporting countries, which have in recent years needed to store tens of billions of dollars but also to have ready access to those funds with minimal market disruption.

The degree to which market size influences inflows of foreign capital is hard to determine. However, the persistence of large capital inflows to the United States despite already large foreign holdings of dollar assets offering modest interest differentials and the disproportionate share of essentially no-risk and high-liquidity U.S. Treasury securities in foreign holdings suggest that the magnitude of flows attributable to the liquidity advantage of U.S. asset markets is probably substantial. Failure of the U.S. government, however, to address its long-term government debt problem could raise concerns about default risk and quickly degrade the attractiveness of Treasury securities to foreign investors, and tend to weaken the dollar.

### U.S. Asset Markets are Often Seen as "Safe Havens"

Many investors may be willing to give up a significant amount of return if an economy offers them a particularly low-risk repository for their funds. The United States, with a long history of stable government, steady economic growth, and large and efficient financial markets, can be expected to draw foreign capital for this reason. The safe-haven-related demand for dollar assets was particularly evident in 2008 (see Figure 1), when uncertainty about global economic and financial conditions caused a substantial "flight to quality" by foreign investors that sharply appreciated the dollar. As global markets stabilized in 2009, the safe haven demand abated somewhat, contributing to the depreciation of the dollar that occurred in the second half of 2009 and during 2010.

The ongoing size of the safe-haven demand for dollar assets is not easy to determine, but the disproportionate share in foreign holdings of U.S. Treasury securities, which markets still consider to be essentially without default risk, suggests that the magnitude of safe-haven motivated flows is probably substantial, capable of periodically exerting sizable upward pressure on the dollar. Again, perceptions of how "safe" dollar assets are likely to be is influenced by how the 112th Congress addresses the federal government's long term debt problem.[12]

### The Dollar is the Principal Global "Reserve Currency"

A reserve currency is a currency held in sizable quantities by foreign governments and central banks as part of their holdings of foreign exchange. Unlike private investors, central banks hold foreign exchange reserves primarily for reasons other than expected rate of return. These so-called official holdings generally serve two objectives. First, the accumulation of a reserve of foreign exchange denominated in readily exchangeable currencies, such as the dollar, provides a safeguard against currency crises arising out of often volatile private capital flows. This is most often a device used by developing economies that periodically need to finance short-run balance of payments deficits and cannot fully depend on international capital markets for such finance. In the wake of the Asian financial crisis of 1997-1998, many emerging economies built up large stocks of foreign exchange reserves, a large share of which were denominated in dollars.

Second, official purchases are used to counter the impact of capital flows that would otherwise lead to unwanted changes in the countries' exchange rates. This is a practice used by China and many east Asian economies that buy and sell dollar assets to influence their exchange rates relative to the dollar in order to maintain the price attractiveness of their exports.

Globally, central bank holdings of reserve currency assets have risen sharply in recent years. The IMF reports that from 2002 through the third quarter of 2010, worldwide official holdings of foreign exchange reserves increased from about $2 trillion to nearly $9 trillion. Given the dollar's status as the dominant international reserve currency, a large portion of the accumulation was of dollar-denominated assets. IMF data indicate that of the $5 trillion of official holdings of which currency composition is known, nearly $3 trillion (or 60%) are in dollar assets. [13] In addition, the U.S. Treasury reports that through January 2011, $3.2 trillion (or 67%) of the $4.5 trillion marketable Treasury securities held by foreigners was being held as foreign official reserves. [14] (The total amount of Treasury securities held by the public, foreign and domestic, through January 2011 was about $9.5 trillion.) [15]

In 2010, China was the world's largest holder of foreign exchange reserves, with holdings valued at more than $2.5 trillion, [16] an increase of about $2 trillion since 2002. The exact currency composition of China's foreign exchange reserves is not made public, but the dollar share is thought to be large because that accumulation is largely the consequence of China's buying dollar assets to stabilize the value of its currency relative to the dollar.

Japan is the second largest holder of foreign exchange reserves, with holdings valued at about $1 trillion; however, these reserves were largely accumulated prior to 2005. [17] Japan has not in recent years actively tried to influence the value of its currency; nevertheless, dollar assets are thought to be a large share of its reserves. But on March 17, 2011, Japan announced that it would, in concert with other Group of 7 (G-7) nations, intervene in currency markets to stabilize the value of the yen.

The Japanese currency had spiked following the earthquake on March 11, 2011, threatening to stall Japan's exports and deliver another blow to an economy already staggered by that disaster. Japanese officials believed that the yen's sudden strength was being driven by speculation that Japan's firms and financial institutions would soon be bringing back a large portion of their overseas investments to fund Japan's reconstruction. The intervention entailed the selling of yen-denominated assets, tending to push down its value relative to other G-7 currencies, such as the dollar. This was the first joint currency intervention by the G-7 countries in over a decade.[18]

Since the third quarter of 2009, however, the total accumulation of dollar assets by foreign central banks has slowed moderately. Of the $1.1 trillion increase in global foreign exchange reserves for the four quarters ending in the third quarter 2010, dollar holdings increased $333 billion, at about half the rate of earlier increases.[19]

## How Will These Determinants Interact to Affect the Dollar?

At any point in time, all of the above factors will exert some amount of upward or downward pressure on the value of the dollar, often pushing in opposite directions, making it difficult to disentangle them from their net effect on the dollar. It is difficult to explain with clarity or predict with precision the dollar's near-term path (i.e., several weeks to several months ahead). However, it is possible to assess the general disposition of the forces (as discussed above) likely to influence the dollar in 2011 and 2012.

The following factors point to near-term depreciation of the dollar:

- Low interest rates and slow economic growth in the United States, particularly in comparison to emerging economies, likely lowers the relative expected rate of return on dollar assets.
- International holdings of dollar assets is high and prudent portfolio management could lead to diversification toward other currencies.
- A substantial trade deficit in goods continues to exert downward pressure on the dollar.
- If concerns about euro area sovereign debt problems abate, this will likely reduce recent safe-haven-motivated inflows for dollar assets.
- A growing inflation problem could induce China to slow accumulation of dollar reserves and let its currency rise relative to the dollar.

# LIKELY EFFECTS OF DOLLAR DEPRECIATION

Standard economic analysis suggests that a sustained depreciation in the value of the dollar in international exchange has several likely effects, positive and negative, on the U.S. economy.

## A Smaller Trade Deficit

The exchange rate determines the relative price of domestic goods and foreign goods, thus it can influence the value and volume of exports sold and imports bought and, in turn, influence the trade balance. Because a depreciating dollar improves the price competitiveness of U.S. exports in foreign markets and deteriorates the price competitiveness of foreign goods in U.S. markets, it will tend to reduce the U.S. trade deficit.[20]

A smaller trade deficit is likely to have two favorable effects on the U.S. economy: first, it will subtract less from demand in the economy, providing a boost to employment; and second, it will slow the growth of U.S. foreign indebtedness. In an economy that still has substantial economic slack, stronger U.S. exports increase domestic economic activity and boost employment; weaker imports represent a rechanneling of domestic spending away from foreign goods and toward domestic goods, which also increases domestic economic activity and boosts employment.

Because the U.S. trade deficit is financed by borrowing from the rest of the world (as evidenced by an equal sized net inflow of foreign capital), a smaller trade deficit will slow the rise of an already substantial net foreign indebtedness and could temper the associated concern about a rising external debt service burden.

The period 1985-1991 was the last time a substantial dollar depreciation and trade deficit adjustment occurred.. At that time, the dollar fell a cumulative 40% from a historically high level. In response, the trade deficit started to narrow within two years of the initial depreciation, falling from 3.5% of GDP to near balance by 1991.

For the period 2002-2007, despite a large depreciation of the dollar, the adjustment process has been much slower, with the trade deficit only tipping down modestly in 2007. However, the depreciation of the dollar was having an impact. Economic research suggests that in the United States, depreciation is likely to have a quicker and stronger impact on exports than on imports.[21] This seems to have occurred. Real (non-petroleum) exports began to accelerate in

2003 (the first full year of dollar depreciation) and would continue to grow at a nearly 10% annual rate through 2006 (the year the trade deficit peaked).[22]

The slow effect of the depreciating dollar on the trade balance was the result of import volumes continuing to grow. Again, economic research suggests that U.S. imports have a relatively muted response to exchange rate changes, with a dollar depreciation more likely to slow their growth rather than cause them to decrease. However, in this period several other factors worked to increase imports above what otherwise might be expected and caused a particularly slow response of the trade deficit to the depreciation of the dollar. First, the rapid shift in trade in recent years toward low-cost emerging economies has tended to erode U.S. price competiveness and offset, in part, the competiveness improving effect of the depreciating dollar. Second, up to 2006 the U.S. economy was growing faster than most other advanced economies, tending to boost U.S. imports. Third, oil prices rose to historic highs, increasing the trade deficits of oil-importing countries, such as the United States. (Because the international price of oil is denominated in dollars, dollar depreciation does not directly affect oil's price in the U.S. market. However, some argue it directly contributes to commodity price inflation. This possible relationship is discussed in the "World Commodity Prices (in Dollars) Tend to Increase" section below.)

The U.S. trade deficit in 2010 increased to $470 billion.[23] The deficit's increase from 2009's recession induced low of $378 billion was to be expected in a recovering economy, as rising economic activity at home and abroad increased goods and asset flows to more normal levels. In particular, the rebuilding of inventories by U.S. businesses, typical in the early stages of economic recovery, drew in a sizable volume of imports. But that process is transitory and likely already substantially completed. With the dollar already at a relatively competitive level and with strong growth occurring in most emerging economies, there may be strong demand for U.S. exports. Barring a major spike in oil prices or an unlikely surge in spending by U.S. consumers, the trade deficit could stabilize for the near-term at about $500 billion. Any further dollar depreciation will give added momentum to exports and will raise the prospect that the trade deficit could fall over the next few years and help to boost the rate of economic growth.

## U.S. International Purchasing Power Decreases

The rising price of imports relative to exports caused by a depreciation of the dollar reduces the purchasing power of U.S. consumers and businesses that purchase imports. To judge the combined effect of export and import price changes on U.S. international purchasing power, economists use the change in the *ratio of export prices to import prices* or what is called *the terms of trade*. For the 26% dollar depreciation that began in early 2002 and ended in mid-2008, the U.S. terms of trade for the same period decreased by approximately 13%.[24]

A 13% decrease in the terms of trade is substantially less than the depreciation of the dollar, which reflects changes in factors in addition to the exchange rate. One factor of particular significance is the effect of changes in producer profit margins. To preserve market share in the U.S. market, importers have shown a tendency to not completely pass through exchange rate depreciations to the dollar price of their products, absorbing a portion of the exchange rate change through slimmer profit margins. This practice substantially mutes the currency depreciation's negative effect on U.S. purchasing power. Also likely muting the impact of a fall in the terms of trade on total purchasing power is the relatively small importance of imports in U.S. gross domestic product (GDP), which only total about 16%.

The dollar value of the loss of purchasing power caused by the dollar's depreciation from 2002 to 2008 can be estimated by comparing the growth of real GDP to the growth of real *command-basis* gross national product (GNP). Command-basis GNP measures the goods and services produced by the U.S. economy in terms of their international purchasing power. In particular, it adjusts the value of real exports to reflect changes in their international purchasing power due to changes in the U.S. terms of trade. Thus, when the terms of trade ratio decreases because of dollar depreciation, real command-basis GNP falls relative to the normally calculated real GDP.[25] From early 2002 through mid-2008, real GDP increased a cumulative $1.9 trillion as compared with command-basis real GDP increasing about $1.6 trillion. The difference of about $300 billion is the estimated loss of international purchasing power due to the dollar's 26% depreciation for that time period.

## U.S. Net External Debt is Reduced

A depreciating dollar tends to improve the U.S. net debt position. This improvement is caused by favorable valuation effects on U.S. foreign assets. These occur because U.S. foreign liabilities are largely denominated in dollars, but U.S. foreign assets are largely denominated in foreign currencies. Therefore, a real depreciation of the dollar increases the value of U.S. external assets and largely does not increase the value of U.S. external liabilities. This asymmetry in the currency composition of U.S. external assets and liabilities means that a dollar depreciation tends to reduce U.S. net external debt.[26]

Exchange rate induced valuation effects are substantial because they apply to the entire stock of U.S. foreign assets, valued at about $18.4 trillion in 2009. The large scale of U.S. foreign assets means that valuation changes can offset a sizable portion of the current account deficit's annual addition to the existing stock of external debt. For example, in 2006, the current account deficit reached a record $811.4 billion. As this was financed by foreign borrowing, it made a like-sized contribution to U.S. external debt. However, the total value of net external debt in 2006 increased only about $300 billion because valuation changes caused the value of the stock of U.S. foreign assets to increase by more than $500 billion. Nearly half of this offset was attributable to positive valuation effects on U.S. foreign assets that were attributable to the dollar's depreciation during that year. In 2007, the impact of valuation changes, including $444 billion caused by dollar depreciation, was sufficiently large to cause the U.S. net external debt to fall despite having to finance a $638 billion current account deficit that year.[27]

## World Commodity Prices (in Dollars) Tend to Increase

The fall of the dollar from 2002 to 2007 coincided with large increases in commodity prices. The price of gold increased from about $300 per ounce to more than $600 per ounce, the price of oil increased from about $20 per barrel to near $140 dollars per barrel, and the index of nonfuel commodity prices rose about 85%.[28] Because most commodities in international markets are priced in dollars, their prices to the U.S. buyer are not directly affected by movements of the exchange rate.

However, a 2008 IMF analysis argues that the dollar does have an indirect impact on commodity prices, that works through at least three channels. First, a dollar depreciation makes commodities, usually priced in dollars, less expensive[29] in non-dollar countries, encouraging their demand for commodities to increase. Second, a falling dollar reduces the foreign currency yield on dollar denominated financial assets, making commodities a more attractive investment alternative to foreign investors. Third, a weakening dollar could induce a stimulative monetary policy in other countries, particularly those that peg their currencies to the dollar. A stimulative monetary policy tends to decrease interest rates, which could stimulate foreign demand, including that for commodities.

The IMF study estimated that if the dollar had remained at its peak of early 2002, by the end of 2007, the price of gold would have been $250 per ounce lower, the price of a barrel of crude oil would have been $25 a barrel lower, and nonfuel commodity prices would have been 12% lower.[30]

Other factors were likely more direct and important causes of the rapid climb of commodity prices at this time. Large increases in world industrial production, particularly in emerging Asian economies, have likely been a factor pulling up commodity prices. Also low interest rates in the United States have reduced the incentive for current extraction over future extraction and generally lowered the cost of holding inventories, dampening the supply response to higher commodity prices.

# OTHER POSSIBLE EFFECTS OF DOLLAR DEPRECIATION

Other impacts of a depreciating dollar are more problematic, but are potential risks.

## U.S. Interest Rates Could Increase

A falling dollar itself does not directly affect interest rates in the United States. However, the underlying international capital flows that influence the dollar may also influence conditions in domestic credit markets. A weakening of the demand for dollar-denominated assets by private investors tends to depreciate the dollar. A weaker demand for dollar assets is also a likely consequence of a decrease in the net inflow of foreign capital to the U.S. economy. Other things equal, a smaller net inflow of foreign capital reduces the supply of loanable funds available to the economy, tending to increase the price of those funds, that is, increase interest rates.

At this time, however, other things are not equal. The economy, while recovering from the 2008-2009 recession, still retains substantial economic slack and the demand for loanable funds by businesses and households remains particularly weak. In addition, at least for the near term, the Federal Reserve appears committed to a policy of monetary stimulus that will keep interest rates low.[31]

However, as economic slack decreases as the recovery progresses, the Fed will likely steadily reduce the amount of monetary stimulus and the domestic demand for credit will likely increase to a more normal level, and together this will exert more upward pressure on interest rates. That pressure will be greater to the degree that domestic savings does not increase sufficiently to offset the reduced inflow of foreign capital (i.e., a reduced supply of loanable funds), making it likely that, coincident with the falling dollar, U.S. interest rates would tend to rise more than they otherwise would.

This added upward pressure on U.S. interest rates could be prevented if there was also an increase in the supply of domestic saving generated by households and the government, sufficient to offset the diminished inflow of foreign capital. Also, rising U.S. interest rates could feedback to improve the relative attractiveness of dollar assets to some foreign investors, tending to slow the net outflow of capital, decrease upward pressure on interest rates, and dampen the rate of dollar depreciation. If, as noted above, the capital outflow is being motivated by other factors in addition to the level of U.S. interest rates, then this feedback effect is not likely to stop the outflow, only slow it.

## Dollar's Reserve Currency Role Could Be Reduced

Foreign central bank holdings of reserve currency assets have risen sharply over the past decade. These "official holdings" have nearly quadrupled since 1997, increasing from about $2 trillion to nearly $9 trillion by the end of 2010. Of the $5 trillion of official holdings of which currency composition is known, nearly $3 trillion (or 60%) is in dollar assets.[32] Euro-denominated assets have the second largest share at about 25%.

For the United States, there are significant benefits from the dollar being the world's primary reserve currency. Central banks' demand for the reserve currency tends to be less volatile than that of private investors. This stabilizes the demand for dollars and reduces the foreign exchange risk faced by U.S. companies in their international transactions. Exchange rate risk is also reduced because the United States borrows in its own currency, so that the appreciation of foreign currencies against the dollar cannot increase debt-service cost or raise default risk. Another major benefit of having the primary international reserve currency is that it enables the United States to borrow abroad at a lower cost than it otherwise could. This cost advantage occurs because there is a willingness of foreign central banks to pay a liquidity premium to hold dollar assets. Also, the dollar's status as the world's reserve currency raises the incidence of foreigners using U.S. asset markets. This added foreign involvement increases the breadth and depth of these markets, which tends to attract even more investors, which further magnifies the benefits of issuing the reserve currency.

However, the prospect of substantial further depreciation of the dollar could erode the dollar's ability to provide the important reserve currency function of being a reliable store of value. Foreign central banks may see the erosion of this function as a growing disincentive for using the dollar as their principal reserve currency. Another potential threat is any perceived unsustainability of the U.S. long-term debt problem that may eventually result in a downgrading of the U.S. sovereign-risk rating.

Yet, so far there appears to be only modest diversification from dollar assets by foreign central banks. The dollar share of official reserves reached a peak value of about 72% in 2001. Over the subsequent decade this share has slowly decreased, stabilizing at about 62% in 2009 and 2010. The principal alternative to the dollar as a reserve currency has been the euro. Since its creation in 1999, the euro share of global official reserves rose from about 18% to 27% in 2007; however, since then the euro has not increased its share of global reserve assets.[33]

Despite the problems posed for some by the dollar's ongoing depreciation, at present there is arguably no alternative currency to assume its role as principal reserve currency. The sovereign debt crisis in Europe is likely to have diminished the euro's attractiveness to central banks. In addition, the size, quality, and stability of dollar asset markets, particularly the short-term government securities market in which central banks tend to be most active, continues to make dollar assets attractive. A further advantage is the power of "incumbency" conferred by the important "network-externalities" that accrue to the currency that is currently dominant. Together these factors will likely inhibit for the medium-term a large or abrupt change in the dollar's reserve currency status. Nevertheless, over the long-term, many economists predict that a multiple currency arrangement is likely to emerge involving, in addition to the dollar, a continued role for the euro and a substantially increased role of China's yuan. This presumes that China will be able to greatly improve the size and liquidity of its financial markets and create attractive financial instruments. Sustained dollar depreciation could accelerate this process by encouraging more active movement away from dollar assets by central banks.[34]

## Risk of a Dollar Crisis Could Be Increased

Although asset market trade offers opportunities to raise overall economic efficiency and improve the economic welfare of borrower and lender alike, trade in assets is prone to occasional volatility, the disorderly resolution of which can lead to financial disruption and, more broadly, a slowing of economic growth. The essential weakness of asset markets is that assets are a claim on a stream of earnings over time—and the future is always uncertain. This can mean that relatively small changes in investors' beliefs about that future could have large effects on the value of the asset. Historically, this has tended to make these markets much more volatile than goods markets, in which value is generally far less contingent on the uncertainties of the future. Add to this the often observed tendency for "herd-like" behavior among investors, particularly those focused on the short run, and the volatility in asset markets can grow larger. Then add in leveraged purchases, the inherent weakness of modern fractional-reserve banking, exchange rate risk, and the usual problems of distance (i.e., different language, law, and business practices) and the potential for volatility and crisis becomes even larger.

There is no precise demarcation of when a falling dollar might move from being an orderly decline to being a crisis, but the depreciation would be significantly more rapid than the orderly fall that has already occurred. The troubling characteristic of a dollar crisis would be that this adjustment could move from orderly to disorderly, due to a precipitous decline in the willingness of investors to hold dollar assets, causing a sharp decrease in the price of those assets and an equally sharp increase in the interest rates attached to those assets. A sudden spike in interest rates could slow domestic interest rate sensitive spending more quickly than the falling dollar can stimulate net exports. This negative impulse could cause overall economic activity to slow, perhaps to the point of stalling the economic recovery.

One factor governing whether dollar depreciation is an orderly or disorderly adjustment is investor expectations about future dollar depreciation. Rational expectations will have a stabilizing effect on the size of international capital flows. The rational forward-looking investor will have some notion of the equilibrium exchange rate and whether the currency is currently overvalued or undervalued. Such investors would only hold assets that have expected yields high enough to compensate for the expected depreciation and also preserve a competitive rate of return.

In contrast, a sharp plunge of the dollar could occur if most investors do not form rational expectations about a likely future depreciation of the dollar. Once investors come to realize that the dollar is falling at a faster rate than they had expected, there could be a sudden attempt by large numbers of investors to sell their dollar assets. But with many sellers and few buyers, the exchange rate would fall precipitously, along with the price of dollar assets, before stabilizing.

Some economists argue that foreign investors do not appear to have built a rational expectation of future dollar depreciation into the nominal yields they are accepting to hold dollar assets. The average nominal rate of return on low-risk treasury securities is currently about 2.5% and in 2010 the dollar depreciated at about a 4% annual rate, so that the ex-post rate of return for foreigners holding these securities has been negative.[35]

If many holders of dollar assets conclude their expectations for dollar depreciation had been too low and try to move quickly out of dollar assets, the ensuing stampede could potentially cause a dollar crisis. A buyer is needed to shed dollar assets, but in a crisis environment this may require a precipitous bidding down of the price of the less desirable dollar assets. This leads not only to a sharply falling exchange rate, but also to sharply rising interest rates in U.S. financial markets (lower-asset prices translate into higher effective interest rates).

The dollar, of course, has been on a depreciating trend since 2002, and foreign investors have continued to hold dollar assets for which the attached interest rate seems insufficient to compensate for that depreciation. But there has been no dollar crisis. The avoidance of crisis is, perhaps, explained in part by the large accumulation of dollar reserves by foreign central banks. If foreign central banks have longer investment horizons than private[36] investors, they will tend to stabilize the demand for dollar assets. In general, the large size and stability of the dollar-asset markets (along with the ongoing needs of central banks and other international investors) for liquidity and a store of value undergirds the strong persistent international demand for dollar assets.[37]

# POLICIES THAT COULD INFLUENCE THE DOLLAR

## Does the United States Have a Dollar Policy?

Treasury Secretaries have in the past asserted that the United States has a "strong dollar policy," but have rarely taken direct steps to influence the dollar's value.[38] As noted earlier, since the 1973 demise of the Bretton Woods fixed exchange rate international monetary system, the de facto U.S. dollar policy has been to let market forces determine the dollar's value. The collapse of that monetary system was to a large degree due to its increasing inability to maintain fixed-exchange rates in the face of the massive growth of international capital flows in a reintegrated and rapidly growing post-war global economy.[39]

Mainstream economic theory suggests that a country cannot be open to large international capital flows (as the United States is) and directly control both its exchange rate and its interest rates. Because the management of interest rates is seen as central to the overriding policy goal of stabilizing the domestic economy to maintain high employment and low inflation, the U.S. Federal Reserve and the central banks of most other advanced economies control interest rates and, therefore, have implicitly decided to let their exchange rates fluctuate, more or less, freely.

The exchange rate, while usually not the primary target, can be affected by macroeconomic policies, such as quantitative easing, fiscal stimulus, and debt reduction. Its movement might well support achieving these broader macroeconomic goals, but a particular level for the exchange rate has not been an explicit policy goal in the United States. However, occasionally the government has acted to directly influence the exchange rate. In addition, government policies, programs, and institutions that undergird a "strong U.S. economy" arguably exert a indirect positive effect on the dollar.

## Policies to Influence the Demand for U.S. Assets

Given the importance of international asset markets in determining the dollar's exchange rate, policies aimed at directly or indirectly influencing the demand and supply of dollar assets would potentially have the greatest direct impact on the dollar.

### *Direct Intervention in the Foreign Exchange Market*

This policy involves the Federal Reserve at the request of the Treasury buying or selling foreign exchange in an attempt to influence the dollar's exchange rate. (This intervention will most often be *a sterilized* intervention that alters the currency composition of the Fed's balance sheet but does not change the size of the monetary base, neutralizing any associated impact on the money supply.) To strengthen the dollar, the Fed could attempt to boost the demand for dollars by selling some portion of its foreign exchange reserves in exchange for dollars. (Sterilization in this case would require the Fed to also purchase a like value of domestic securities to offset the negative effect on the monetary base of its selling of foreign exchange reserves.)

The problem with intervention is that the scale of the Fed's foreign exchange holdings is small relative to the size of global foreign exchange markets, which have a *daily* turnover of more than $4.0 trillion.[40] Facing markets of this scale, currency intervention by the Fed would likely be insufficient to counter a strong market trend away from dollar assets and prevent depreciation of the dollar.

A coordinated intervention by the Fed and other central banks would have a greater chance of success because it can increase the scale of the intervention and have a stronger influence on market expectations. Since 1985, there have been six coordinated interventions: the Plaza Accord of 1985 to weaken the dollar, the Louvre Accord of 1987 to stop the dollar's fall, joint actions with Japan in 1995 and 1998 to stabilize the yen/dollar exchange rate, G-7 action in 2000 to support the newly introduced euro, and G-7 action in 2011 to limit appreciation of the Japanese yen. All but the Louvre Accord do correspond with turning points for the targeted currencies.

However, these interventions were most often accompanied by a change in monetary policy that was consistent with moving the currencies in the desired direction. Many economists argue that coordinated intervention in these circumstances played the useful role of a signaling device helping overcome private investors' uncertainty about the future direction of monetary policy and the direction the central banks want the currency to move. But absent an accompanying change in monetary policy it is unlikely that even coordinated intervention would be successful at altering the exchange rate's trend if it were being strongly propelled by private capital flows.

## Monetary Policy

The Federal Reserve uses monetary policy to influence economic conditions. By increasing or decreasing interest rates, it tightens or loosens credit conditions.

Changing the level of interest rates can also influence the dollar's exchange rate. A tighter monetary policy would tend to strengthen the dollar because higher interest rates, by making dollar assets more attractive to foreign investors, other things equal, boosts the demand for the dollar in the foreign exchange market. In contrast, lower interest rates would tend to weaken the dollar by reducing the attractiveness of dollar assets. In either case, however, it would be unprecedented for the Fed to use monetary policy to exclusively target the exchange rate, but it could be the side-effect of policies aimed at controlling inflation or stimulating aggregate spending to speed economic recovery.

In general, a floating exchange rate gives the central bank greater autonomy to use monetary policy to achieve domestic stabilization goals. In the current macroeconomic situation, if the Fed were obligated to prevent the dollar from depreciating, it would likely be constrained from applying the degree of monetary stimulus needed to promote economic recovery.

It is likely that the Fed's current policy of monetary stimulus to sustain economic recovery, by keeping interest rates low, has exerted downward pressure on the dollar as well. Although not the primary target of this monetary policy, the incidental depreciation of the dollar contributes to the Fed's stabilization goal of boosting economic growth by providing a boost to net exports.

## Fiscal Policy and Federal Debt

Government choices about spending and taxing can also influence the exchange rate. Budget deficits tend to have a stimulative effect on the economy. However, because the government must borrow funds to finance a budget deficit, it increases the demand for credit market funds, which, other things equal, tends to increase interest rates. Higher interest rates will tend to increase the foreign demand for dollar-denominated assets, putting upward pressure on the exchange rate.

However, in the current state of the U.S. economy, with a sizable amount of economic slack and weaker than normal private demand for credit market funds, current government borrowing does not appear to have elevated market interest rates, and, therefore, does not appear likely to exert upward pressure on the exchange rate. Moreover, the likely prospect of a slower than normal economic recovery suggests a substantial amount of economic slack and relatively weak private demand for credit is likely to persist over the near term. These conditions will continue to mute the interest elevating effect of currently anticipated government borrowing and continue to exert minimal upward pressure on the dollar.

As economic recovery moves the U.S. economy closer to full employment and the private demand for credit market funds increases, continuing large government budget deficits may result in higher interest rates. Some foreign investors could be attracted by these higher interest rates, increasing their demand for dollar assets. This would exert upward pressure on the dollar.

However, if the federal government does not implement a credible solution to its long-term debt problem, it is possible that the expectation of persistent large budget deficits and sharply rising public debt could degrade the expected long-term performance of the U.S. economy by crowding out productive investment and slowing the pace of economic growth. This anticipated deterioration could reduce international investors' expected rate of return on dollar assets, accordingly reduce the long-term demand for dollar assets. This reduced demand would exert downward pressure on the dollar's international exchange value.

Putting in place a creditable program of fiscal consolidation would also have an ambiguous effect on the dollar's longer-term path. Less government borrowing would tend to lower interest rates and depreciate the dollar, while the improved prospect for long-term growth and expected rates of return would tend to appreciate the dollar.

## Policies to Increase the Demand for U.S. Exports

Policies that tend to increase the foreign demand for U.S. goods and services also tend to strengthen the dollar.

### *Lower Foreign Trade Barriers*

The continued existence of various trade barriers in many countries may keep the demand for U.S. exports weaker than it otherwise would be. If lowering those barriers significantly boosts the demand for U.S. goods and services, it would also exert some upward pressure on the dollar exchange rate. It is difficult to judge how strong this upward pressure would be. Moreover, this is not likely to be a readily implementable policy tool and probably has little near-term significance for the dollar's exchange rate.

*Support for Development of New Products*

If the United States has goods and services that are strongly in demand in the rest of the world, there will be some upward pressure on the exchange rate. Economic theory suggests that the government's role in this process is to support those aspects of research and development that are likely to be under-invested in by the private market. This type of policy would most likely have long-run implications, but not have much effect on the near-term value of the dollar.

## Indirect Government Influence on the Dollar

Over the long run, at least three factors will likely continue to indirectly support the international demand for dollar assets: (1) the basic economic performance of the U.S. economy as measured by GDP growth, productivity advance, and pace of innovation has for the past 25 years been superior to that of Japan and the major euro area economies;[41] (2) the Fed is widely seen as a credible manager of monetary policy and has a strong record of maintaining macroeconomic stability; and (3) the large and highly liquid U.S. asset markets will likely continue to be an attractive destination for foreign investors. Therefore, decisions by the 112th Congress regarding policies that enhance or degrade any of these three attributes of the U.S. economy will accordingly tend to indirectly strengthen or weaken the dollar's long-term path. Of likely immediate relevance is the near term issue of sustaining economic recovery and reducing unemployment and the long-term issue of reducing the growth of federal debt.

## GLOBAL IMBALANCES, THE DOLLAR, AND ECONOMIC POLICY

As already discussed, the dollar's exchange rate largely reflects fundamental economic forces, particularly those that influence the demand for and supply of assets on international financial markets. Currently, an examination of those forces highlights a large and potentially destabilizing imbalance in the global economy: in the United States persistent large trade deficits and the accumulation of foreign debt, and in the rest of the world large trade surpluses, weak domestic demand, and the accumulation of dollar denominated assets. Most economists would argue that this is a condition that carries more than a negligible risk of generating financial instability and eventual global economic crisis.

To achieve an orderly correction of these imbalances that assures more stable exchange rates and leaves all the involved economies on sounder macroeconomic footing, mainstream economic thinking suggests that the needed rebalancing can be most efficiently achieved by a coordinated international policy response, the salient elements of which are

- in the United States, raising the national saving rate via substantial increases in the saving rates of households and government and through that reducing the U.S. trade deficit to a "sustainable" size;[42]
- in Japan and Europe, generating faster economic growth primarily propelled by domestic spending rather than net exports;
- in Asia (excluding Japan and China), fostering a recovery of domestic investment and reducing the outflow of domestic saving; and
- in China (and other surplus economies that fix their exchange rates to the dollar), allowing their currencies to appreciate and channel more of their domestic savings into domestic spending.[43]

A key attribute of such a rebalancing of global spending would likely be further depreciation of the dollar. This outcome illustrates that an orderly depreciation of the dollar can be, on balance, a beneficial attribute of policy adjustments and economic changes that would ultimately improve economic conditions in the United States and abroad. There is some evidence that a global rebalancing is in progress. In the United States, the saving rate of households is up and the federal government seems to be moving toward raising public saving by reducing its long-term deficit problem. In China, the yuan has appreciated and the government's recently released five-year plan points to that country undertaking policies to raise its domestic consumption and narrow its global trade surplus.[44]

## End Notes

[1] The trade-weighted exchange rate index used is the *price-adjusted broad dollar index* reported monthly by the Board of Governors of the Federal Reserve System. The real or inflation-adjusted exchange rate is the relevant measure for gauging effects on exports and imports. A trade-weighted exchange rate index is a composite of a selected group of currencies, each dollar's value weighed by the share of the associated country's exports or imports in U.S.

trade. The *broad* index cited here is constructed and maintained by the Federal Reserve. The *broad* index includes the currencies of 26 countries comprising 90% of U.S. trade and, therefore, the broad index is a good measure of changes in the competitiveness of U.S. goods on world markets.

[2] See CRS Report RL33577, *U.S. International Trade: Trends and Forecasts*, by Dick K. Nanto and J. Michael Donnelly for more data and charts on exchange rates.

[3] Data on bilateral exchange rates are available at Board of Governors of the Federal Reserve System, *Federal Reserve Statistical Release H.10*, http://www.federalreserve.gov/releases/h10/hist/.

[4] The current account is a tally of international purchases (imports) and sales (exports), and the current account balance measures the country's net exports of goods and services. The capital account is a tally of international purchases and sales of dollar denominated assets, and the capital account balance measures the country's net foreign investment. If the capital account is in surplus, foreigners are investing more in the United States then Americans are investing abroad, leading to a net inflow of capital. Because every purchase of a foreign good or asset requires the payment of a domestic good or asset, net flows in the current account and the capital account will be equal and offsetting. Therefore a current account deficit must be matched by an equal capital account surplus, and a current account surplus by a capital account deficit. The exchange rate adjusts to make this so.

[5] See U.S. Department of Commerce, Bureau of Economic Analysis, *U.S. International Economic Accounts*, 2007, Table 1, http://www.bea.gov/international/bp_web/list.cfm?anon=71&registered=0.

[6] The G-7 refers to the periodic Group of Seven finance ministers and central bank governors conference. The seven countries represented are Canada, Japan, France, Germany, Italy, the United Kingdom, and the United States.

[7] International Monetary Fund, World Economic Outlook, *Global Imbalances: In a Saving and Investment Perspective*, September 2005, pp. 100-104.

[8] Prudent investment practice counsels that the investor's portfolio of asset holdings have not only an appropriate degree of *diversification* across asset types, but also diversification across the currencies in which the assets are denominated. Moving from a relatively undiversified investment portfolio to a more diversified one spreads risk, including exchange rate risk, across a wider spectrum of assets and helps avoid over- exposure to any one asset.

[9] U.S. Department of the Treasury, *Report on Foreign Portfolio Holdings of U.S. Securities*, Table 1, May 13, 2010, http://www.treasury.gov/resource-center/data-chart-center/tic/Documents/shl2009r.pdf.

[10] IMF, *Global Financial Stability Report*, October 2010, Statistical Appendix, Table 3, http://www.imf.org/External/Pubs/FT/GFSR/2010/02/pdf/statappx.pdf.

[11] Federal Reserve Bank of New York, *Primary Dealer Transactions in U.S. Government Securities*, February 23, 2011, http://www.newyorkfed.org/markets/statistics/deal.pdf.

[12] On the demand for safe assets see Ben S. Bernanke, 'International capital flows and the returns to safe assets in the United States 2003-2007, *Financial Stability Review*, Banque de France, no. 15, February 2011, http://www.banque-france.fr/gb/publications/telechar/rsf/2011/etude02_rsf_1102.pdf.

[13] In contrast, the United States in this time period held foreign exchange reserves of less than $200 billion on average, with annual increments of only $1 billion to $10 billion. See IMF, Currency Composition of Official Foreign Exchange Reserves, December, 2010, http://www.imf.org/external/np/sta/cofer/eng/cofer.pdf.

[14] U.S. Department of the Treasury, Treasury International Capital System (TIC), *Major Foreign Holders of Treasury Securities,* http://www.treasury.gov/resource-center/data-chart-center/tic/Documents/mfh.txt.

[15] U.S. Department of the Treasury, Treasury Direct, *Dept to the Penny,* http://www.treasury.gov/resource-center/datachart-center/tic/Documents/mfh.txt.

[16] Statistics on Chinese international reserves are from Chinability, a nonprofit provider of Chinese economic and business data, http://www.chinability.com/Reserves.htm.

[17] Japan, Ministry of Finance, February 28, 2011, http://www.mof.go.jp/english/e1c006.htm.

[18] Binyamin Appelbaum, "Goup of 7 to Intervene to Stabilize the Yen's Value," *New York Times* March 17, 2011, http://www.nytimes.com/2011/03/18/business/global/18group.html.

[19] IMF, *Currency Composition of Official Reserves*, December 30, 2010, http://www.imf.org/external/np/sta/cofer/eng/cofer.pdf.

[20] This effect is likely to be evident first on real trade flows (the volume of exports and imports) and more slowly on nominal trade flows (the current dollar value of exports and imports). This differential effect on real and nominal flows occurs because the higher relative price of imports has two impacts. On the one hand, domestic consumers buy a reduced volume of foreign goods, while on the other hand, each unit of the foreign goods is valued higher in terms of dollars. Initially, the volume effect can be dominated by the value effect, causing the nominal trade balance to not fall or perhaps even rising for a period in response to a depreciating exchange rate. Ultimately, the volume effect could come to dominate the value effect and the nominal trade deficit would also begin to fall.

[21] International Monetary Fund, *World Economic Outlook September 2007,* Chapter 3, "Exchange Rates and the Adjustment of External Imbalances."

[22] U.S. Census Bureau, *U.S. International Trade Data,* http://www.census.gov/foreign-trade/statistics/historical/realpetr.pdf.

[23] Bureau of Economic Analysis, *U.S. International Transactions Account,* Table 1, line 77, http://www.bea.gov/international/bp_web/simple.cfm?anon=71&table_id=1&area_id=3.

[24] Bureau of Economic Analysis, *National Economic Accounts, Table 1.8.6,* http://www.bea.gov/national/nipaweb/SelectTable.asp?Selected=N.

[25] Ibid.

[26] Most countries are not able to borrow in their own currency, so a fall of their exchange rate will tend to increase their net external debt. This was a problem that plagued the economies caught in the Asian financial crisis in 1997, when their crashing currencies ballooned the home currency value of their external debt.

[27] Data for U.S. net external debt are compiled annually and the most recent estimate is for 2009. Data for 2010 is scheduled to be released in July 2011. For further details on net external debt and valuation effects see U.S. Department of Commerce, Bureau of Economic Analysis, *U.S. Net International Investment Position,* July 2010, http://www.bea.gov/international/index.htm#bop.

[28] IMF Primary Commodity Prices, February 2011, http://www.imf.org/external/np/res/commod/Table1-020911.pdf.

[29] Assuming their currency is not pegged to the dollar.

[30] International Monetary Fund, *World Economic Outlook – April 2008*, pp. 48-50.

[31] Board of Governors of the Federal Reserve System, Monetary Policy Report to the Congress, March 1, 2011, http://www.federalreserve.gov/monetarypolicy/mpr_20110301_part1.htm.

[32] IMF, Currency Composition of Official Foreign Exchange Reserves, December, 2010, http://www.imf.org/external/ np/sta/cofer/eng/cofer.pdf.

[33] Ibid, IMF.

[34] For further discussion of this issue, CRS Report RL34083, *The Dollar's Future as the World's Reserve Currency: The Challenge of the Euro*, by Craig K. Elwell.

[35] U.S. Department of the Treasury, *2010 Average Historical Monthly Interest Rates*, http://www.treasurydirect.gov/govt/rates/pd/avg/2010/2010.htm.

[36] Robert A. Mundell, "Capital Mobility and Stabilization Policy," *Canadian Journal of Economics and Political Science, 29(4)*, 1963, pp 475-485.

[37] For more discussion of this issue, see CRS Report RL34311, *Dollar Crisis: Prospect and Implications*, by Craig K. Elwell.

[38] See for example Keith Bradsher, *New York Times,* August 17, 1995, "Treasury Chief Says Strong Dollar Isn't a Threat to Trade," http://www.nytimes.com/1995/08/17/business/international-business-treasury-chief-says-strongdollar-isn-t-a-threat-to-trade.html; *USA Today*, August 1, 2006, " New Treasury secretary backs strong dollar, Social Security solution", http://www.usatoday.com/money/economy/2006-08-01-paulson-speech_x.htm; and Tom Patrino, *Los Angles Times*, November 12, 2009, " Treasury Secretary Tim Geither pays lip service to keeping dollar strong," http://articles.latimes.com/keyword/lip-service.

[39] On post-war global capital flows and the demise of the Bretton Woods system, see Barry Eichengreen, *Globalizing Capital: A History of the International Monetary System*( Princeton University Press, 1996), pp. 93-135.

[40] Bank of International Settlements, *Triennial Central Bank Survey of Foreign Exchange and OTC Derivatives Market*, September 11, 2010, http://www.bis.org/press/p100901.htm.

[41] The World Economic Forum in its 2010 *Global Competitiveness Report* ranks the United States as the fourth most competitive economy in the world and the United States has been at or near the top of this ranking since it began in 1979, http://www3.weforum.org/docs/WEF_GlobalCompetitivenessReport_2010-11.pdf.

[42] A trade deficit is arguably sustainable if it does not cause the U.S. foreign debt/GDP ratio to rise. For the United States a trade deficit as a percent of GDP of 2% or less would probably meet this sustainability criterion. For further discussion of sustainability see CRS Report RL33186, *Is the U.S. Current Account Deficit Sustainable?*, by Marc Labonte.

[43] On global rebalancing, see for example: Olivier Blanchard, *"Sustaining Global Recovery,"* International Monetary Fund, September 2009, http://www.imf.org/external/pubs/ft/fandd/2009/09/index.htm; "Rebalancing," The Economist, March 31, 2010, http://www.economist.com/node/15793036; and Board of Governors of the Federal Reserve System, Vice-chairman Donald L. Kohn, Speech "Global Imbalances," May 11, 2010, http://www.federalreserve.gov/ newsevents/speech/kohn20100511a.htm.

[44] *China Daily,* October 28, 2010, "China's Twelfth Five-Year Plan signifies a new phase in growth," http://www.chinadaily.com.cn/bizchina/2010-10/27/content_11463985.htm and Martin Feldstein, "The End of China's Surplus, *Project Syndicate,* January 28, 2011, http://www.project-syndicate.org/commentary/feldstein32/English.

In: Dollar Depreciation
Editor: Lachlan S. Roy

ISBN: 978-1-61470-692-2
© 2011 Nova Science Publishers, Inc.

**Chapter 2**

# DOLLAR CRISIS:
# PROSPECT AND IMPLICATIONS[*]

## *Craig K. Elwell*

## SUMMARY

The dollar's value in international exchange has been falling since early 2002. Over this five year span, the currency, on a real trade weighted basis, is down about 25%. For most of this time the dollar's fall was moderately paced at about 2.0% to 5.0% annually. Recently, however, the slide has accelerated, falling about 9% between January and December of 2007. An acceleration of the depreciation brings the periodic concern of an impending dollar crisis to the fore. There is no precise demarcation of when a falling dollar moves from being an orderly decline to being a crisis. Most likely it would be a situation where the dollar falls, perhaps 15% to 20% annually for several years, and sends a significant negative shock to the U.S. and the global economies. A crisis may not be an inevitable outcome, but one that likely presents considerable risk to the economy.

The large U.S. current account deficits are sustained by an inflow of foreign capital. That inflow also exerts upward pressure on the value of the dollar as investors demand dollars to enable the purchase of dollar denominated assets. There is a limit to how much external debt even the U.S. economy can incur. Erasing the U.S. trade gap would stop the

---

[*] This is an edited, reformatted and augmented version of a Congressional Research Service publication, CRS Report for Congress RL34311, dated May 6, 2008.

accumulation of debt. This would occur through a rebalancing of global spending, composed of a decrease of domestic spending in the United States and an increase of domestic spending in the surplus economies. Such shifts in domestic spending patterns must be induced by a depreciation of the dollar, causing the price of foreign goods to rise for U.S. buyers and the price of U.S. goods to fall for foreign buyers.

The critical factor governing whether orderly and disorderly adjustment of international imbalances occurs is foreign investor expectations about future dollar depreciation. Rational expectations will have a smoothing effect on the size of international capital flows. In contrast, a sharp plunge of the dollar is likely to occur if investors do not form rational expectations. If the dollar then depreciates at a rate faster than foreign investors now expect, a dollar crisis becomes likely. Currently foreign investors do not appear to have a realistic expectation of future dollar depreciation. A dollar crisis could start when they realize their error and try to move quickly out of dollar assets — the likely stampede would cause a "dollar crisis." Three prominent counter-arguments to the dollar crisis prediction (the *global savings glut* argument, the *Bretton Woods II* argument, and the *economic dark matter* argument) do not offer credible alternatives to the dollar crisis outcome.

The transition to a new equilibrium of trade balances may not be smooth, likely involving a slowdown in economic activity or a recession. The ongoing U.S. housing price crisis raises the risk of a dollar crisis causing a recession. With fiscal policy most likely out of consideration in the near term, the task of attempting to counter the short-term contractionary effects of a dollar crisis would fall upon the Federal Reserve. A stimulative monetary policy can be implemented quickly but its eventual effectiveness is uncertain. The most useful policy response by foreign economies would be complementary expansionary policies to offset the negative impact of their appreciating currencies on their net exports. Attempts to defend a currency against this crisis driven appreciation would be costly and likely fail.

# INTRODUCTION

The dollar's value in international exchange has been falling since early 2002. Over this five-year span, the currency, on a real trade-weighted basis, is down about 25%.[1] This depreciation has been orderly so far. For most of this, time the dollar's fall was moderately paced at about 2.0% to 5.0% annually. Recently, however, the slide has accelerated, falling over 9.0% between January and December of 2007, but falling faster over the last four months than during the previous seven months. For the first three months of 2008 the dollar has fallen another 2.9%

An acceleration of the depreciation brings the periodic concern of an impending dollar crisis to the fore. There is no precise demarcation of when a falling dollar moves from being an orderly decline to being a crisis. Most likely it would be a situation where the dollar falls, perhaps 15% to 20% annually for several years, and sends a significant negative shock to the U.S. and the global economies. This crisis may not be an inevitable outcome, but one that likely presents considerable risk.

That negative shock will likely lead to some degree of slowing of economic activity. For the U.S. economy, already weakened by the ongoing housing price crisis, a further dampening effect caused by a plummeting dollar would significantly raise the risk of recession. For the rest of the world, the impact would also depend on what else was going on in their economies at the time of the dollar's fall. It is likely that the negative impact would be substantial for foreign economies that are highly dependent on export sales to the United States. [2]

This concern about the dollar's near-term path raises three questions: (1) will a dollar crisis occur? (2) what macroeconomic impact might a dollar crisis have on U.S. economy, and the world economy? and (3) are there policy responses that can counter adverse impacts?

## ANATOMY OF DOLLAR CRISIS

The large U.S. current account deficits are sustained by an inflow of foreign capital. The necessary counterpart for this inflow to occur is economies in the rest of the world that generate capital outflows and run trade surpluses. The country with a trade deficit is an international borrower and is accumulating external liabilities. The economies with trade surpluses are international lenders and accumulate external assets.

The capital inflow to the United States also exerts upward pressure on the value of the dollar as investors demand dollars to purchase dollar denominated assets. The upward demand pressure on the value of the dollar is pulling against the downward pressure on the dollar exerted by the large supply of dollars pumped into the foreign exchange markets by the U.S. trade deficit. From the mid-1990s until early 2002, the strength of foreign demand for dollar assets was sufficient to keep the dollar appreciating despite the rapid expansion of the trade deficit in this time period. Since 2002, however, although the United States continued to receive a rising inflow of capital, the strength of the associated demand for dollars has not been sufficient to prevent the dollar from depreciating moderately under the weight of large current account deficits in this time period.[3]

This external financing of the U.S. current account deficit has occurred with relative ease so far. But large scale borrowing can not go on indefinitely. There is a limit to how much external debt even the U.S. economy can incur. Currently, the U.S. debt/GDP ratio is at a historical high of about 19.2%. It is uncertain how much higher this ratio can go, but most economists would argue that there is an upper bound and at some point the US. trade deficit will need to be closed to stabilize the level of external debt at a feasible level.

Erasing the U.S. trade gap will require a rebalancing of global spending. A trade deficit is a symptom of an economy that spends more than it produces; therefore, rebalancing requires a decrease of domestic spending in the United States. In contrast, a trade surplus is a symptom of an economy that spends less than it produces; therefore, rebalancing requires an increase of domestic spending in surplus economies. These shifts in domestic spending patterns can be induced by a decrease in the price of U.S. goods and services relative to the price of foreign goods and services. For the change in relative prices to happen the dollar must fall, causing the price of foreign goods to rise for U.S. buyers and the price of U.S. goods to fall for foreign buyers. In addition to the downward pressure on the dollar of the large trade deficit, an important animating force in this adjustment would likely be a reduction in the demand for dollar denominated assets by foreign investors and a shrinking of the associated capital inflow.

This rebalancing of global spending does not have to be disorderly and disruptive. The major depreciation of the dollar that followed the breakup of the Bretton Woods international monetary system in the early 1970s was largely orderly. More recently, the protracted fall of the dollar and reduction of the U.S. trade deficit in the late 1980s and early 1990s was also an orderly adjustment of international economic imbalances.

Why might a disorderly adjustment and dollar crisis occur? The critical factor is foreign investor expectations about future dollar depreciation. Economic theory indicates that a rational foreign investor in deciding whether to hold more or continue to hold his current dollar assets will build into that decision some estimate of future dollar deprecation. For example, a dollar asset and a euro asset each of similar risk and each offering a 2% real return would present very different *expected* returns if the dollar is expected to depreciate 4% annually and the euro to remain steady over the holding period.

With these expectations, the rational investor would need the dollar asset to offer a real yield in excess of 6% to make it more attractive then the euro.asset at 2%.

A moderation of market behavior and crisis free adjustment occurs when foreign investors develop rational expectations about the currency's future path. Rational expectations about the dollar's future path will have a smoothing effect on the size of international capital flows. In a time of capital inflows, some expectation of possible future depreciation tends to moderate those inflows. Conversely, in a time of capital outflows, some expectation of possible future appreciation will tend to moderate those outflows.

In contrast, a sharp plunge of the dollar is likely to occur if investors do not form rational expectations about the dollar's future path. If the dollar then depreciates at a rate faster than foreign investors now expect, a dollar crisis becomes likely. The rate of depreciation of the dollar that is rational to expect is the rate which is consistent with avoiding the accumulation of an unsustainable level of U.S. external debt. It is, however, difficult to say what that debt level is. Nevertheless, there is a debt/GDP ratio that prudent economic agents will judge to be an upper bound. Given that, the question becomes: what rate of dollar depreciation will give a rate of closure of the trade deficit that contains the debt/GDP ratio below that upper bound?

The economist Paul Krugman has calculated a range of estimates of U.S. external debt accumulation under alternative rates of convergence of the trade deficit to balance.[4] He assumes, based on the general consensus of experts, that a further real depreciation of the dollar of about 35% would, at a minimum, be necessary to close the U.S. trade gap.[5] He then considers two rates of convergence to this goal: one occurring over 20 years with a 1.75% annual rate of depreciation of the dollar. It leads to an external debt/ GDP ratio of 118%. At that size it is possible that a third or more of the U.S. capital stock would be foreign owned. The second scenario has convergence occurring over 10 years with an annual rate of depreciation of the dollar of about 3.75%. It leads to an external debt/GDP ratio of 58%, which is more than twice the size of the current historically high level of U.S. debt/GDP ratio. That seems high for a large, relatively closed economy like the United States, but, perhaps, plausible given the current trends in financial globalization.

Guarding against an overly pessimistic outcome, these computations incorporate significant constraints on the growth of the external dept/GDP ratio. For instance, each estimate of the eventual debt to GDP ratio assumes that nominal GDP will grow at an annual rate of 5.5%, with a combination of 3.0% real GDP growth and 2.5% inflation rate. This could be a slightly optimistic assumption for the pace of real GDP growth, which has averaged only 2.7% in the current economic expansion. Slower growth of GDP would make the Debt/GDP ratio climb faster.

Also, Krugman's external debt estimates take into account the tendency of a depreciating dollar to improve the U.S. net debt position. This improvement is caused by favorable valuation effects on U.S. foreign assets. These occur because U.S. foreign liabilities are largely denominated in dollars, but U.S. foreign assets are largely denominated in foreign currencies. Therefore, a real depreciation of the dollar increases the value of U.S. external assets and largely does not increase the value of U.S. external liabilities. This asymmetry in the currency composition of U.S. external assets and liabilities results in a dollar depreciation reducing U.S. net external debt.[6]

Exchange rate induced valuation effects are substantial because they apply to the entire stock of U.S. foreign assets, valued at near $14 trillion in 2006. The large scale of U.S. foreign assets means that valuation changes can offset a sizable portion of the current account's deficits annual addition to the existing stock of external debt. For example, in 2006, the current account deficit made a $811.4 billion contribution to U.S. external debt. But the total value of net external debt in 2006 increased only about $300 billion due to an offset of over $500 billion (over 60%); nearly half of this offset was attributable to positive valuation effects on U.S. foreign assets caused by the dollars depreciation that year.[7] If rapid dollar depreciation causes significant numbers of future lenders to be only willing to hold nondollar denominated U.S. debt the scale of the positive valuation effects would shrink and make the debt/GDP ratio climb faster.

In addition, one could argue that the 35% real depreciation target understates what is needed to close the current account deficit. For the United States, the equilibrium exchange rate is probably a moving target, and one whose path has been uneven but on balance has fallen over the past 30 years. This secular decline is thought to be rooted in rising technology in emerging economies that has allowed them to generate a steady rise in exports that compete with U.S. tradable goods. It is difficult to predict the pace of this secular decline, but during the 10- to 20-year convergence period used in this analysis, it is possible that reaching the equilibrium exchange rate will require more than the exercise's assumed 35% real depreciation of the dollar.

Taken together, these considerations probably give Krugman's computations of the implied rise of the debt/GNP ratios a bias toward understatement. Nevertheless, the scale of the U.S. trade imbalance that needs to be eliminated causes the estimated ratio to soar in either alternative. If these estimates are understated, then even more rapid real depreciation would be needed to erase the trade deficit and keep the debt to GNP ratio below a realistic upper bound.

Based on these computations, Krugman argues that a rational foreign investor would have to expect the dollar to depreciate by, at least, about 2% per year and very likely depreciate by 4% per year or more. Do holders of U.S. assets appear to have taken this probable depreciation into account? It appears they have not. Using estimates of real long-term interest rates in the United States, the euro area, and Japan, Krugman finds no difference in real yield between the U.S. and euro area assets, and about a 1 percentage point advantage for U.S. assets over Japan's assets.

This lack of a real interest rate spread between dollar assets and similar foreign assets indicates that investors are expecting virtually no depreciation of the dollar over the holding period. Therefore, in the face of a seemingly inevitable depreciation of the dollar at 2% or faster, these investors are holding U.S. assets that offer, in terms of their own currency, a zero or negative real return.

When foreign investors come to realize their error and try to avoid large capital loses by moving quickly and substantially out of dollar assets, the dollar will fall precipitously and the dollar crisis begins. As the dollar's fall gains momentum there are likely to be negative interactions with domestic financial markets and domestic economic activity that will add to this downward momentum, overcoming, for awhile, the usual corrective mechanisms.

In a dollar crisis, it is unlikely that the current account deficit could decrease as rapidly as foreign investors would desire to curtail the inflow of capital to the United States. But the current account deficit will have to be financed. This economic necessity will generate strong economic forces to assure that the needed economic adjustments, at home and abroad, occur. The necessary macroeconomic adjustments will be discussed in a subsequent section of the report. At this point it will be useful to consider possible counter arguments to a dollar crisis happening.

# POSSIBLE REASONS WHY
# A DOLLAR CRISIS WON'T OCCUR

Over the last few years, several arguments that offer reasons why the U.S.trade deficit is more sustainable and a dollar crisis less likely than presented in Krugman's analysis have received serious consideration in policy discussions about the U.S. trade deficit and the associated rise of U.S. external debt. This section evaluates three prominent counterarguments to the dollar crisis prediction: the *global savings glut* argument, the *Bretton Woods II* argument, and the *economic dark matter* argument.[8]

## Global Savings Glut

Ben Bernanke, now chairman of the Federal Reserve Board, has argued that there exists outside of the United States a large excess of global saving relative to global investment opportunities.[9] These large and growing flows of foreign saving are the result of the rapid economic growth of many emerging economies and large oil earnings by petroleum exporting countries. The IMF estimates that developing countries had a net capital outflow of about $720 billion in 2006. A large share of these funds are not going to be used in the home economy and are attracted to U.S. asset markets because they offer excellent wealth storage services. This service encompasses the ability of U.S. asset markets to offer a combination of reasonable rates of return, safety, and high liquidity. The result has been unusually large capital inflows to the United States.

These inflows of capital have kept U.S. interest rates low and have exerted strong upward pressure on the value of dollar. It is argued that this saving glut could continue to grow for many years into the future. Therefore, it will continue to enhance the sustainability of the U.S. trade deficit and, in turn, provides sustained and substantial upward pressure on the value of the dollar. This persisting inflow does not preclude depreciation of the dollar but would moderate the depreciation and greatly reduce the risk of a dollar crisis.

While the existence of a global savings glut can help explain why the large U.S. trade deficit has been sustained with relative ease well beyond what many experts had expected, it does not avoid the looming reality of there being an upper-bound on U.S. net external debt. And, that this debt ceiling creates the inevitable need for a large real depreciation of the U.S. dollar. A saving glut can explain why global real interest rates are low. But it does not avoid the problem posed by those rates being as low as rates in both the United States, a deficit country, and the surplus economies.

This anomaly occurs because foreign investors in dollar assets are not taking into account the impending need for a sustained and substantial real depreciation of the dollar. When this risk becomes apparent to those investors, they will hurry to find other destinations for their savings. If that happens, the dollar would plummet.

## Bretton Woods II

Some economists have characterized the current global monetary arrangement as Bretton Woods II (BWII).[10] The first Bretton Woods (BWI) was the global monetary arrangement in place from the end of World War II through 1973. BWI was a formal system of fixed exchange rates centered on the dollar. Other countries were obliged to maintain their currencies value relative to the dollar. When needed, this adjustment was accomplished by foreign central banks buying or selling foreign exchange to keep their currencies' value at the fixed parity with the dollar. The speculative crises caused by relatively free flowing international capital that plagued the inter-war years were to be prevented by strict controls on the flow of capital between economies. This system worked reasonably well in the early post-war period. But accumulating pressure for a major dollar devaluation and increasingly porous capital controls led to its breakdown in the early 1970s. Since 1973, most major economies have allowed their currencies to, more or less, float freely on the global foreign exchange markets, allowing its exchange value to be driven by the international supply and demand for its goods and assets. Capital controls were also largely abandoned by these nations.

BWII is not a formal arrangement or organization. It is a de facto arrangement whereby central banks, particularly in Asia, amass dollar reserves so as to stabilize their currencies value relative to the dollar. This stabilization is achieved by the central banks buying dollar assets sufficient to keep their currencies from rising relative to the dollar. It is also supported by the BWII economies imposing significant controls on capital flows to and from their economies. Not letting their currencies rise relative to the dollar enables them to maintain the competitiveness of their exports in the U.S. market and perpetuate a successful development strategy driven by export-led growth.

China has been a important participant in this arrangement, with its central bank in recent years amassing well over $1 trillion in foreign exchange reserves, a large proportion being various dollar assets.

With China at its center, it could be argued that because BWII has been a very successful development strategy for China, and because that country still has over 300 million nonindustrial workers to absorb into its industrial and service sectors, this de facto monetary arrangement will endure for many more years, and continue to exert strong upward pressure on the value of the dollar, countering any tendency towards a dollar crisis.

However, serious questions can be raised about the stability of BWII.[11] One potential problem is that such large scale accumulations of foreign exchange reserves can have disruptive macroeconomic and financial effects on the accumulating economy. To prevent the foreign exchange reserves from causing an unwanted increase the country's money supply, its central bank must *sterilize* the accumulation of foreign currency assets. It does this by purchasing compensating amounts of domestic assets which pulls money out of the economy.

Sterilization of dollar inflows on such a large and growing scale, however, will be an increasingly difficult task for China and other emerging economies. They have small and immature asset markets that are unlikely to be able to continue to effectively sterilize further large scale reserve growth. It is likely that this foreign liquidity will begin to leak into their domestic economy and push up the money supply. This would, in turn, lead to increased inflation and a domestic lending boom that generates asset price bubbles. This could cause significant disruptions in their weak financial markets and adversely affect their economic activity.

In addition, the balance sheets of the foreign central banks that hold large amounts of dollar assets are exposed to large losses if the dollar crashes. Collectively, the BWII central banks have an incentive to hold on to their dollar assets to preserve the value of these holdings. Individually, however, the BWII central banks have an incentive to sell their dollar assets if they suspect the dollar will soon plunge. Therefore, the stability of BWII is highly dependent on how much cooperation there is among these central banks.

Further, a large share of the capital inflow to the United States comes from private investors whose economic incentives are different than those of the BWII central banks. Perhaps foreign private investors remain heavily in dollar assets because they think that BWII can prevent a dollar crash. But there is no strong basis for such a belief. The efficacy of BWII would be evident if at some point it had demonstrated an ability to sustain the dollar's value despite an outflow from the United States of private capital motivated by realistic expectations about the dollar's future falling path. But, what has been occurring are large official inflows along with large private inflows that are accepting a real return that is insufficient to compensate for the expected rate of fall of the dollar which realistically must occur.

If BWII is to offset the outflow of private capital based on realistic expectations of the dollar's future path, the BWII central banks would need to increase their already huge dollar reserves by an amount that is probably not feasible. And the problem posed by there being an upper bound to the U.S. debt/GNP ratio would still remain. BWII seems unlikely to be seen as a reliable barrier to a plummeting dollar once foreign investors see the need to adjust to more realistic expectations of the dollar's future path.

## Dark Matter

Another perspective on the U.S. international balances has been presented by the economists Ricardo Hausmann and Frederico Struzeneggar.[12] It is their contention that there are large measurement errors in the U.S. trade data that cause a big understatement of U.S. exports and, in turn, a big overstatement of the size of U.S. net external debt. In their opinion this error is of a magnitude that the current account balance has actually been in surplus in recent years and that the United States is an external net creditor, not a debtor. The principal evidence of this is that despite a seeming huge net external debt the United States has consistently run a sizable surplus in the investment income portion of the current account.

The unmeasured exports are not picked up in the export data because they are are services hidden within U.S. capital outflows. Once abroad, these assets generate an income stream that is measured as investment income in the current account data.

These invisible assets have been named *dark matter* because they, like the astronomical phenomenon, have a visible effect — generating investment income — that is caused by unseen service exports. It is contented that the dark matter effect is large. With proper accounting, it transforms a net debt position of about $2.5 trillion to a net surplus position of about $600 billion.

Three classes of invisible exports are said to exist: global liquidity services, global insurance services, and knowledge services. The three exports, in turn, are attached respectively, to three types of capital outflows: U.S. currency, U.S. sovereign debt, and U.S. foreign direct investment.

### Liquidity Services

This service is derived from the U.S. currency's special status as a global source of liquidity. A large portion of the $700 billion Federal Reserve Notes in circulation are held abroad. Estimates of the share vary from a low of 30% to a high of 70%. The holding of this currency by foreigners is equivalent to an interest free and irredeemable loan to the United States with an implicit value of as much as $25 billion.

### Insurance Services

It is argued that the world economy uses low-risk U.S. Treasury Securities to fill out the low-risk end of their investment portfolios. Much like a global bank, the United States can then use these proceeds to invest in higher yielding bonds from emerging economies. This amounts to the world exchanging a risky asset for a safe asset and the yield difference is the equivalent of an insurance premium the world pays the U.S. for lowering its risk.

### Knowledge Services

This service is said to occur because U.S. foreign direct investment embodies a host of unmeasured assets. These services are in the form of know-how, brand recognition, expertise, and research and development. This is the form of dark matter that proponents see as the most important.

The major implication of the dark matter argument for the dollar is that because the true state of the U.S. trade position is not precarious and because the United states is not a net external debtor, there is no need for a dollar depreciation to keep the debt to GNP ratio within bounds. Foreign investors could be quite willing to hold more dollar assets despite their having little apparent yield advantage over foreign assets. The risk of a dollar crisis in this circumstance would be small.

Although there is probably some merit to the dark matter argument, most economists would argue that the scale of the effect is vastly smaller than claimed by its proponents. For that reason, economic dark matter probably does little to forestall the need for a substantial correction of the U.S. trade deficit. And that correction must be set in motion by a substantial real depreciation of the dollar, beyond the depreciation that has already occurred, and that will persist for several years.

# THE MACROECONOMIC EFFECTS OF A DOLLAR CRISIS

In the standard macroeconomic model, a reduction of foreign capital inflows would have no long-term effect on aggregate spending and output. A real depreciation of the dollar would encourage U.S. export sales and discourage domestic spending on imports, *increasing net exports* and shrinking the trade deficit. At the same time foreigner's reduced willingness to hold dollar assets will reduce the inflow of foreign capital, pushing down the price of U.S. securities, and pushing up U.S. interest rates. Higher interest rates would then induce a *decrease in interest sensitive spending* such as residential investment, consumer durables, and business investment. In the end, the trade deficit would be gone, the composition of U.S. spending and output would change, but there would not be any change in the total level of spending and output.

The transition to this new equilibrium of trade balances, however, may not be smooth. Some argue that there could be a very rough transition involving a sharp slowdown in economic activity or a recession. Substantial near-term slowing of economic activity would occur if the decrease of U.S. domestic spending occurs more quickly then the increase of U.S. net-exports. Interest sensitive purchases tend to be more postponable then other domestic spending and would likely fall relatively quickly as interest rates spiked. Net exports' response could be significantly slower. The peak effect on net exports in response to a currency depreciation is usually about two years later. However, in this situation the scale of adjustment needed to eliminate the trade deficit is unusually large and will involve large shifts of resources into the production of tradable goods which take time. This could slow the response of net exports further.

What aggravates this situation and significantly adds to the risk of a dollar crisis triggering a recession is the U.S. economy's ongoing burden of adjusting to the housing price crisis. Falling home prices reduce household wealth, discouraging household spending, and dampen aggregate spending. As with most markets, there is a self correcting mechanism that facilitates beneficial adjustment in the housing market. This occurs as weaker aggregate demand also weakens the demand for credit and causes interest rates to decrease. By stimulating interest sensitive spending, falling interest rates, other things equal, arrest some of the downward impulse on aggregate demand of falling housing prices.

However, if the economy must also endure the disruptive effects of a plummeting dollar, other things would not be equal. In a dollar crisis, great numbers of foreign investors are attempting to sell large amounts of dollar assets at the same time causing dollar asset prices to fall sharply and interest rates to rise sharply. Interest rates will continue to rise until a sufficient number of dollar-averse investors can be enticed to offer enough capital to finance the slowly shrinking current account deficit. An interest rate spike like this is likely to forestall any ameliorating effect of otherwise falling interest rates on the housing crisis, slowing aggregate demand more than would otherwise occur.

In this environment, where two crises exert downward pressure on aggregate spending, the risk rises that the short-term adjustment of the U.S. trade balance could involve a much quicker and much larger slowing of domestic spending with so little near-term boost from rising net exports. This magnified near-term negative impact could be sufficient to cause a recession.

# THE RESPONSE OF ECONOMIC POLICY

The ability of conventional fiscal and monetary policy, here and abroad, to counter the near-term contractionary effects of a dollar crisis is problematic.

## Response of U.S. Economic Policy

When the government budget is in deficit, it reduces domestic saving and when in surplus it increases domestic saving. Therefore, conceptually an infusion of government saving caused by policy actions that reduce the federal budget deficit could compensate for the dwindling flow of foreign savings stemming from foreign investors move out of dollar assets. Governments adding to the domestic flow of saving would tend to decrease interest rates and stimulate aggregate spending. This would also mean that the trade balance adjustment could occur with out a reduction of domestic investment. An outcome, that bodes better for productivity and the longterm growth of the U.S. living standard.

However, to get to this point there would first be an initial dampening effect flowing from the government's budget deficit reducing actions of spending less, taxing more, or doing both. In the short run, a negative fiscal impulse in conjunction with the already occurring short-run negative effects of the housing crisis and dollar crisis would amplify the recession risk. Also, the impulse toward lower interest rates would mute the self-correcting effect of a rising interest differential between dollar assets and foreign assets that would otherwise help to slow the dollar's fall.

Again, conceptually the short-term negative effects of fiscal tightening on aggregate spending could be countered by a complementary short-term monetary stimulus which spurs spending through exerting downward pressure on interest rates. In practice, however, whether alone or in tandem with monetary policy, the use of budget deficit reduction as a policy response to the near-term problems of a dollar crisis is improbable. The necessary tax and spending changes are unlikely to be implemented quickly enough. Over a longer time horizon, where fiscal action may be more likely, increased government saving from budget deficit reduction would prevent the dwindling inflows of foreign saving from causing an undesired compression of U.S. domestic investment.

With fiscal policy most likely out of consideration in the near-term, the task of attempting to counter the short-term contractionary effects of a dollar crisis would fall upon the Federal Reserve. It would most likely do this by pumping liquidity into the economy and exerting downward pressure on interest rates. Monetary policy can be implemented quickly and its favorable effect felt with a modest time lag. Nevertheless, there are some potential constraints on the Fed's ability to follow a stimulative monetary policy during a dollar crisis.

One potential constraint is a consequence of the dollar depreciation inducing a increase in U.S. inflation by causing the price of U.S. imports' to rise sharply. This inflation effect will be muted by import's relatively small share of final demand. Also many foreign producers will, to preserve market share, prevent a full pass-through of the exchange rate change to the price of their products exported to the United States. Nevertheless it is still possible that the scale of dollar depreciation in a crisis could lead to a 1 to 2 percentage point jump in the inflation rate. This inflation effect would stop once the dollar stabilized. But to prevent this inflation spurt from generating an increase in inflation expectations and causing a more enduring run-up of inflation, the Fed might be reluctant to validate those expectations by continuing to provide monetary stimulus.

Another possible constraint on fully pursuing policy of monetary stimulus is that if the fall of the dollar is seen by the Fed to be too extreme, policy action may be needed to gain some control over the falling currency. Most likely this would involve changing direction and increasing interest rates to entice foreign investors back to dollar assets.

Even if the Fed does not relent in applying monetary stimulus, the traditional channel for doing this is by targeting short-term interest rates, usually the nominal federal funds rate. However, that rate can only be decreased to zero. With the nominal federal funds rate already down to about 2.0%, there is a question of whether sufficient monetary stimulus could be applied before this rate reaches the so-called zero bound.

At this point, there are nontraditional ways that might be used to implement monetary policy. These include targeting longer-termed federal securities, making direct loans to banks, or altering inflation expectations (i.e., lowering real rates via a credible commitment to higher future inflation) that could be used. It is still uncertain, however, if these untried alternative monetary policy levers are effective and, if effective, whether that effect can be delivered to the economy quickly enough to counter the sharp short-term negative impulse to domestic spending of a fast falling dollar.

## Response of Foreign Economic Policy

The economic policy response of other economies, particularly those with trade surpluses, could help or hinder the macroeconomic adjustment forced by a dollar crisis. As discussed earlier, a falling dollar (and rising foreign currencies) is the instrument that will lead to a rebalancing of world spending. For economies with trade surpluses the rebalancing would manifest as a increase of domestic spending and decrease of net exports.

As was true for the United States, after the rebalancing has been completed, affected foreign economies total spending and level of output would be unchanged. The negative effects from the decrease in net-exports caused by their currencies appreciation will be counter-balanced by the positive effect from lower interest rates, pushed down by increased capital inflows, boosting domestic spending. Like the United States, however, the rest of the world's near-term transition to this new equilibrium might not be smooth, and also carry an elevated risk of recession.

Many U.S. trading partners have relied on export sales to the American market as their principal, or at least their major, engine of economic growth. This practice is most overt in those economies that tie their currency to the dollar so that dollar depreciation does not reduce the price competitiveness of their exports. In a dollar crisis, there could be a temptation to try to continue to prevent their currencies from appreciating against the dollar. Defending their currencies would slow the global adjustment. But it is unlikely to be successful policy, however, in the face of a global attempt to move out of dollar assets and a plummeting dollar. The likely aftermath of such an attempt would be that these economies would be left holding an even larger stock of dollar assets whose value is a fraction of what it was when purchased.

The deflationary impact of a rising currency would help economies, such as China, that are facing an inflation problem. On the other hand, it could cause problems for a country like Japan that still teeters on the edge of deflation.

In general, a more useful policy response by foreign economies would likely be expansionary economic policies sufficient to boost domestic spending and offset the near-term negative impact of an appreciating currency on their net exports. Because this stimulus must be applied quickly for it to be effective, the task would most likely be undertaken by the monetary authorities.

As was true for the United States, it is problematic whether the application of a stimulative monetary policy by the central banks of the surplus economies would have sufficient positive effect on aggregate spending in the near-term to avoid a strong downward push on global economic activity. In economies that are already facing a significant inflation problem, such as China, there could be a reluctance to fan the inflationary flames any further by undertaking added monetary expansion. In any event, a cooperative policy response by the United States and its major trading partners would certainly help to smooth the global adjustment to a dollar crisis.

## CONCLUSION

Predicting the path of exchange rates is always an endeavor with an above normal level of uncertainty. Nevertheless, it seems undeniable that a further sizable depreciation of the dollar is necessary in the long run to keep the United States' large and growing external debt within realistic bounds. It is difficult, however, to predict how global investors who hold the U.S. external debt will respond to the seemingly large erosion of the value of those dollar assets caused by this inevitable depreciation of the dollar.

A rational response to holding a currency unable to perform its role as a store of value would be to move quickly into assets denominated in other more stable currencies. Yet, despite the sizable depreciation of the dollar that has already occurred, foreign investors continue to hold dollar assets. There are reasons, in addition to the store of value function, to hold those assets. Safety and liquidity are two other important reasons, both functions that the wide and deep dollar asset markets perform very well. Also, many investors pursue very long term goals and could be willing to ignore short run risk. It seems unlikely, however, that these other reasons for holding dollar assets, would continue to trump the dollar's rapidly dwindling ability to provide the store of value function. If so, then a sharp dollar fall could be just ahead.

A plummeting dollar would have positive and negative effects on the world economy as well. Eventually the positive and negative impacts on the level of economic activity should be offsetting, but it would leave the world economy with more stable external balances. But, there is reason to be concerned that in the short-run the negative effects may be dominant, raising the risk of recession.

The triggering of a recession by a plummeting dollar will depend on what else is going on in the economy when the currency crashes. If already weakened by other forces, the risk of recession would grow much larger. If generally good economic conditions prevail, then economic activity is likely to slow in the near-term but avoid a recession.

It is important to take into consideration that the U.S. economy is large and resilient, and able to absorb substantial shocks without necessarily transmitting a significant adverse effect on overall economic activity. In contrast, a dollar crisis could send a more devastating economic blow to economies that are highly dependent on exporting to the U.S. market to sustain their economic growth.

# End Notes

[1] The trade-weighted exchange rate index used is the *real broad index* reported monthly by the Board of Governors of the Federal Reserve System.

[2] For an early treatment of the dollar crisis scenario, see Stephen Marris, *Deficits and The Dollar: World Economy at Risk*, Institute for International Economics, Washington DC, 1985.

[3] For a more extensive discussion of international asset flows and the trade deficit, see CRS Report RL31032, *The U.S. Trade Deficit : Causes, Consequences, and Cures*, by Craig K. Elwell.

[4] Paul Krugman, "Will There Be a Dollar Crisis," *Economic Policy*, July 2007.

[5] See, for example, Micheal Obstfeld and Kenneth Rogoff, "Global Current Account Imbalances and Exchange Rate Adjustment," *Brookings Papers on Economic Activity*, no. 1, 2005.

[6] Most countries are not able to borrow in their own currency so a fall of their exchange rate will tend to increase their net external debt. This was the problem that plagued the economies caught in the Asian financial crisis in 1997, when their crashing currencies ballooned their external debt to such a degree that they became insolvent.

[7] For further details on net external debt and valuation effects see U.S. Department of Commerce, Bureau of Economic Analysis, *U.S. Net International Investment Position*, July 2007.

[8] Paul Krugman, "Will There Be a Dollar Crisis," *Economic Policy*, July 2007, also examines these arguments.

[9] See Ben Bernanke, "The Global Savings Glut and the U.S. Current Account Deficit," the Sandbridge Lecture, Virginia Association of Economics, March 10, 2005; and CRS Report RL33140, *Is the U.S. Trade Deficit Caused by a Global Saving Glut*, by Marc Labonte.

[10] Michael P. Dooley, David Folkerts-Landau, and Peter Garber, *An Essay on the Revived Bretton Woods System*, NBER Working Paper 9971, 2003.

[11] Neil Roubini and Brad Sester, "Will the Bretton Woods II Regime Unravel Soon? The Risk of a Hard-Landing in 2005-2006," presented at Symposium sponsored by the Federal Reserve Bank of San Francisco and the University of California, Berkeley, San Francisco, 2005.

[12] Ricardo Hausmann and Federico Sturzenegger, "U.S. and Global Imbalances: Can Dark Matter Prevent the Big Bang?," (Kennedy School of Government, Harvard University, Unpublished Working Paper: Cambridge, 2005) and CRS Report RL33570, *U.S. External Debt: How Has the United Sates Borrowed Without Cost*, by Craig K. Elwell

In: Dollar Depreciation
Editor: Lachlan S. Roy

ISBN: 978-1-61470-692-2
© 2011 Nova Science Publishers, Inc.

*Chapter 3*

# THE DOLLAR'S FUTURE AS THE WORLD'S RESERVE CURRENCY: THE CHALLENGE OF THE EURO[*]

## *Craig K. Elwell*

## SUMMARY

Globally, central bank holdings of reserve currency assets have risen sharply in recent years. These "official holdings" have nearly tripled since 1999 to reach $5 trillion by the end of 2006. Nearly $3 trillion has been amassed by developing Asia and Japan. China, in particular, now has official reserves that exceed $1 trillion. In addition, the oil-exporting countries have increased their official reserves by about $700 billion. The dollar's status as the dominant international currency has meant that as much 70% of this large accumulation of official reserves are of some form of dollar asset.

There are significant advantages for the United States in having the dominant reserve currency. These advantages include reduced exchange rate risk and lower borrowing costs. However, these large accumulations of dollar assets in foreign official holdings also means that foreign central banks have become important participants in and influences on U.S. financial markets and the wider U.S. economy.

---

[*] This is an edited, reformatted and augmented version of a Congressional Research Service publication, CRS Report for Congress RL34083, dated July 10, 2007.

Four factors — share of world output and trade, macroeconomic stability, degree of financial market development, and network externalities — combine to influence the choice of a reserve currency. The euro has improved its standing in all four areas but the dollar retains significant advantages. Available data show only modest diversification from dollar assets by foreign central banks from the time of the euro's introduction in 1999 through the end of 2006. The dollar's share of total official reserves rose through the 1990s, reaching a peak value of about 72% global reserves in 2001. By 2003 that share fell to about 66% and remained near that level through 2006. The euro's share of global official reserves rose from about 18% in 1999 to 25% in 2003, but has remained near this level through 2006.

Looking to the future, the dollar's status as the dominant reserve currency may be challenged by the euro because it increasingly offers many of the advantages of the dollar but fewer of the risks. The dollar's most important advantage is the size, quality, and stability of dollar asset markets, particularly the short-term government securities market where central banks tend to be most active. The high liquidity of these financial markets makes the dollar an excellent medium of exchange. A further advantage is the power of "incumbency" conferred by the "network-externalities" that accrue to the currency that is dominant. Together these factors make it unlikely there will be a large or abrupt change in the dollar's reserve currency status.

However, the euro is seen by some as poised to challenge the dollar in the store of value function of a reserve currency. The sheer magnitude of dollar assets in the official reserves of foreign central banks and the realistic prospect of continued, and perhaps disorderly, depreciation of the dollar against most currencies, place central banks at considerable risk of incurring large capital losses on their dollar asset holding. With more than enough dollar reserves to meet liquidity needs, prudent asset management would seem to dictate some diversification away from the dollar and toward the euro.

# THE RISING INTERNATIONAL IMPORTANCE OF "OFFICIAL HOLDINGS"

Central bank holdings of reserve currency assets have risen sharply in recent years. These "official holdings" have nearly tripled since 1999 to reach $5 trillion by the end of 2006. These large accumulations of reserves have been concentrated among countries with large global current account surpluses. Nearly $3 trillion has been amassed by developing Asia and Japan. China, in particular, now has official reserves that exceed $1 trillion. In addition, the oil-exporting countries have increased their official reserves by about $700 billion.[1]

The dollar's status as the dominant international currency has meant that as much as 70% of this large accumulation of official reserves is held in some form of dollar asset. The U.S. Treasury reports that through mid-2005, 34% of the more than $3 trillion outstanding marketable Treasury securities was being held in foreign official reserves. (All foreign holdings, official and private, amount to 52% of all outstanding Treasury securities.)[2] These large accumulations of dollar assets in foreign official holdings mean that foreign central banks have become important participants in U.S. financial markets, as well as in the wider U.S. economy.[3]

For the United States, there are significant benefits to being the world's reserve currency. Central banks' demand for the reserve currency tends not to be as volatile as that of private investors. This stabilizes the demand for dollars and reduces the foreign exchange risk faced by U.S. companies in their international transactions. Exchange rate risk is also reduced because the United States borrows in its own currency so that the appreciation of foreign currencies against the dollar cannot increase debt service cost or raise default risk.

Another major benefit of being the primary international reserve currency is that it enables the United States to borrow abroad at a lower cost then it otherwise could. This cost advantage occurs because there will be a willingness of foreign central banks to pay a liquidity premium to hold dollar assets.

Also, the dollar's status as the world's reserve currency raises the likelihood of foreigners using U.S. asset markets. This added foreign involvement increases the breadth and depth of these markets, which then tends to attract even more investors, which then continually magnifies the benefits of being the reserve currency.

Since 2003, sharply rising capital inflows from foreign central banks have financed on average about 50% of the U.S. current account deficit, increasing the sustainability of the trade deficit by compensating for a sizable weakening of private capital inflows.[4] It is estimated that these recent official reserve accumulations have kept U.S. long-term interest rates from 0.5 to 1.0 percentage points lower than otherwise.[5]

Historically, a single currency has been the dominant reserve currency. In the 19th century sterling played this role, succeeded by the dollar in the 20th century. As the 21st century has begun to unfold the dollar has remained the dominant international currency. But the euro, created in 1999 as part of the

European monetary union (EMU), has been seen by some economists as a potential challenger to the dollar's dominant position as an international currency in the $21^{st}$ century.[6]

To the degree that the euro displaces the dollar in the official holdings of central banks, the benefits to the United States of the dollar as a reserve currency will be reduced. The viability of the euro as a substitute for the dollar will hinge on several factors that determine how well it can perform the necessary roles of a reserve currency for a central bank.

## THE ROLES OF A RESERVE CURRENCY

An international currency is one used by non-residents to accomplish the three standard roles of any currency: be a medium of exchange, a unit of value, and a store of value. However, for central banks these three roles serve different needs than those of the private investor:

- The *medium of exchange* function serves the need for foreign exchange intervention as central banks attempt to counter unwelcome changes in the value of their domestic currency caused by private inflows and outflows of capital.
- The *store of value* function serves the need for reserve accumulation as self-insurance against periodic balance of payments crisis and as a public demonstration of commitment to exchange rate stability.
- The *unit of account* function serves the need of some countries for a monetary anchor to bolster domestic monetary policy in combating inflation.

Typically, the currency used as the medium of exchange will also serve as the main store of value. Also, because of the large scale of recent reserve holdings, some central banks may turn more attention to the currency's ability to also provide the store of value function of concern to private investors — steadiness of asset value and rate of return.

The already large holdings of dollar assets and the prospect of continued depreciation of the dollar's exchange rate are likely to be seen by foreign central banks as major disincentives for using dollars as their principal reserve currency. In contrast, the appreciation of the euro exchange rate and the substantial increase in the liquidity of the euro caused by the improvement in the breath and depth of euro financial markets since 1999 raises the attractiveness of the euro as a reserve currency.

## FOUR FACTORS INFLUENCING CHOICE
## OF A RESERVE CURRENCY

Economists have identified four factors that will jointly influence how well a currency can serve central banks as a medium of exchange, as a store of value, and as a unit of account.

First, the larger a country's share of world output and trade the more likely it is that other countries will use it as a monetary anchor or in external transactions. This factor tends to raise the likelihood that other countries will hold liabilities denominated in its currency and therefore tends to also hold more of its assets in the same currency. The euro is probably not at any sizable disadvantage relative to the dollar in this category.

Second, macroeconomic stability, particularly price stability, is needed to establish confidence in the currency's value. Without this confidence a currency's ability to play its role as a unit of account and as a store of value is undermined. The dollar's status in this category may be eroded by the prospect of long-term exchange rate depreciation.

Third, a high degree of financial market development, offering large size and high liquidity, makes it more likely that a country's currency will be used by foreign central banks as the medium of exchange for currency intervention. Also, a broad and deep financial sector tends to reinforce overall economic stability. In this area, the dollar has been singularly attractive. But the development of euro area financial markets has advanced steadily since its 1999 introduction.

Fourth, network externalities create a self-generating demand for a dominant currency. The more often a currency is used as a medium of exchange, the more liquid it becomes and the lower are the costs of transacting in it, leading, in turn, to it becoming even more attractive to new users. Network externalities create a tendency toward having one dominant currency and confer a substantial *incumbency advantage* to the dollar over the euro.[7]

None of these influences on the choice of a reserve currency is likely to change quickly, acting to make any shift in the status of the dominant reserve currency a slow process, with substantial changes most often emerging over decades.[8]

# THE CURRENT CURRENCY COMPOSITION
## OF OFFICIAL RESERVES

Data on the currency composition of official reserves is imperfect. The most comprehensive source is the International Monetary Fund's (IMF) currency composition of foreign exchange reserves (COFER) database.[9] Included in this series are monetary authorities' claims on non-residents in the form of banknotes, bank deposits, treasury bills, short-term and long-term government securities, and other claims usable to meet balance of payments needs. However, COFER data do not include the holdings of currency by the issuing country. Also, the COFER data only provides national currency specific information for about 70% of total global reserves because the reserves of many emerging economies are missing from the tally. Despite these limitations, the COFER data will most likely reveal basic trends in holdings of the dollar and euro in global official reserves.

The COFER data show only modest diversification from dollar assets by foreign central banks from the time of the euro's introduction in 1999 through the end of 2006. The dollar's share of total official reserves was at its lowest point in the early 1990s at about 45%. Through the 1990s that share rose, in large measure because of accumulation of dollar reserves by emerging economies, reaching a peak value of about 72% global reserves in 2001. By 2003, that share fell to about 66% and has remained near this level through 2006. The euro's share of global official reserves rose from about 18% in 1999 to 25% in 2003, but has remained near this level through 2006.

Again, the source of much of the change in both the level of official reserves and their distribution among currencies was central banks in developing countries, accounting for 58% of the growth of total foreign exchange holdings in this period, and also decreasing their share of dollar holdings from 70% to 60%, and increasing their share of euro holdings from 19% to 30%. In contrast, among industrial economies the dollar share of holdings held steady and the share of euro holdings increased modestly.

Another interesting change in the 1999-2006 period was a fall in the share of yen assets in official reserves (down from 6% to 3%) and a rise in the share of pounds sterling (up from 2.7% to 4.4%). This relatively small increase in the international status of the pound may be insignificant by itself, but could very significant for the status of the euro if the United Kingdom were to join the EMU.

# EURO VS. DOLLAR

In the framework of the three functions of a reserve currency: being a medium of exchange, a store of value, and a unit of account, how does the euro stack-up against the dollar?[10]

## As a Medium of Exchange

This is typically the most important one to be fulfilled by any well functioning currency. For central banks, this role will revolve around use of the currency for intervention in foreign exchange markets. Intervention is a task that places a premium on liquidity, the capability — on short notice, possibly in adverse conditions — of turning assets quickly into cash with little or no impact on the asset's price. The liquidity of a currency in both foreign exchange markets and asset markets is important.

In foreign exchange markets, the Bank of International Settlements' (BIS) most recent *Triennial Survey of Foreign Exchange and Derivatives Markets* shows that on April of 2004 the euro entered on one-side of 37% of all foreign exchange transactions. The dollar's share of transactions on foreign exchange markets fell from 94% in 1998 to 89% in 2004.[11]

In asset markets, central banks invest in instruments with limited risk, making conditions in the country's government security markets the most relevant for the choice of an intervention currency. The attractiveness of the euro has been increased by the formation of the EMU, creating the world's second largest government securities market. In 2005, the outstanding stock of government securities of the several euro area governments totaled $4.7 trillion. This compares to $4.2 trillion of outstanding U.S. treasury securities. Suggesting that more than size may matter, the largest government securities market is Japan, but the holding of yen-denominated reserves has declined in recent years.

Despite the greater size and rising attractiveness of the euro area's government securities market, the U.S. Treasury market has several advantages that continue to enhance its attractiveness to foreign central banks. First, the short-term segment of the U.S. Treasury market, composed of about $950 billion U.S. Treasury bills with terms of three months to one year, is about twice as large as the euro area counterpart. Treasury bills are a low risk and highly liquid instrument that are well suited to the reserve currency needs of central banks.

Second, U.S. Treasury securities have a single issuer and the euro area has twelve. The several issuers of euro assets are not of uniform credit worthiness. U.S. Treasury securities carry a AAA credit rating but some euro area economies government securities have a lower credit rating.

Third, the U.S. Treasury market appears to offer far greater liquidity than the euro area government securities markets. One indicator of this is a daily turnover in U.S. government securities markets of nearly $500 billion. Japan is second largest at $150 billion per day. Turnover is an indicator of how easily a market can absorb large transactions without changing the asset's price. The superior (small) bid-ask spreads found in the U.S. government securities market are further evidence of their very high liquidity.

## As a Unit of Account

In official use this role is largely linked to the selection of an exchange rate as a monetary anchor. In recent years, the euro has increased in importance in fulfilling this role. In 2004, the IMF reported that out of 150 pegged currencies, 40 used the euro as an anchor currency. However, because of incomplete reporting, this type of tally may understate the true degree of attachment — "gravitational pull" — of one currency to another.

An alternative approach is to examine the actual co-movements of currencies to determine how closely currency's track the euro and the dollar. This currency sensitivity evidence suggests that the euro's gravitational importance is rising. European countries outside of the EMU, such as Switzerland, Sweden, Norway, as well as eastern and central Europe move very closely with the euro. In Latin America, as well, there is evidence of the increasing gravitational pull of the euro, particularly in Brazil and Chile. One other, very notable change has been for the traditional dollar-influenced currencies of Australia, Canada, and New Zealand mirroring from one-half to two-thirds of the euro's movement. In contrast, the currencies of emerging economies in Asia generally follow the dollar quite closely.

Thus, while the dollar is still the most important currency as a monetary anchor, the euro has become a viable international competitor to the dollar in its role as a unit of account for central banks. However, some caution in judging the degree of convergence is called for because the depreciation of the dollar since 2002 makes it difficult to separate temporary changes from permanent changes. Have central banks moved away from the dollar as a monetary anchor only until the dollar stabilizes again or has the structure of demand for the currency changed permanently?

## As a Store of Value

The critical criterion for a currency to be a good store of value is the ability to maintain real purchasing power over time. That ability will be closely tied to a country pursuing stable and sustainable macroeconomic policies. Although the United States has in recent years consistently maintained vigorous economic growth and relatively low inflation, large current account deficits and the prospect of substantial and, perhaps, disorderly depreciation of the dollar's exchange value may erode the dollar's ability to serve as an international store of value.

Since early 2002, the dollar has fallen in value by about 30% or about 5% per year. That depreciation more or less erases any positive yield on treasury securities held by foreign central banks. The bilateral comparison shows even greater depreciation against certain currencies, with the dollar down 11% against the euro in 2006 alone. The ultra-high liquidity of U.S. asset markets has perhaps provided sufficient advantage to compensate for the eroding effect of the depreciating dollar on the rate of return on dollar assets.

But, because the large scale of worldwide official holding seems to exceed the amount needed for intervention purposes, central banks may begin to focus more on expected rate of return and less on liquidity in managing their holdings. Nominal rates of return have been generally higher on dollar assets than euro assets, however, expected depreciation of the dollar relative to the euro likely erases this advantage. Therefore, with the steady growth in the depth and breadth of euro area asset markets providing investment alternatives to the dollar, there is likely to be a rising incentive for central banks to use a greater share of the more stable euro to meet their store of value objectives.

However, diversification away from the dollar by central banks may be constrained by the need to maintain a balance between the currency composition of their assets and its countries' external liabilities because many countries borrow in dollars. Asset-liability currency balance, particularly for emerging economies, tends to reduce the prospect for balance sheet mismatches in times of crisis and improves the foreign investors evaluation of the country's credit worthiness. Data for emerging market economies for the 2003-2005 period show the dollar's share of external liabilities to be about 66% and its share of reserves assets to be only 59%. In contrast, the euro's share of external liabilities was 24% and share of reserves was 31%. Therefore, by this criterion the dollar is under represented in official reserves and the euro is over represented.

In addition, it is possible to diversify across asset types within a particular currency so as to improve likely risk adjusted returns. There has been an increase in foreign official holdings of U.S. agency bonds, particularly mortgage backed securities issued by Fannie Mae and Freddie Mac, and U.S. corporate bonds, according to the New York Fed. Given the typically conservative investment behavior of most central banks, there is likely only limited scope for this type of diversification.

# CONCLUSION

The dollar's status as the dominant reserve currency may be challenged by the euro because it increasingly offers many of the advantages of the dollar but fewer of the risks. Nevertheless, the dollar retains significant advantages. The most important advantage is the size, quality, and stability of dollar asset markets, particularly the short-term government securities market where central banks tend to be most active. The high liquidity of these financial markets makes the dollar an excellent medium of exchange for foreign central banks.

A further advantage is the power of "incumbency" conferred by the important "network-externalities" that accrue to the currency that is currently dominant. Together these factors make it unlikely there will be a large or abrupt change in the dollar's reserve currency status.

However, the euro does seem poised to challenge the dollar in the store of value function of a reserve currency. The sheer magnitude of dollar assets in the official reserves of foreign central banks, and the prospect of continued sizable, and perhaps disorderly, depreciation of the dollar against most currencies, places central banks at considerable risk of incurring large capital losses on their dollar asset holding. With more than enough dollar reserves to meet liquidity needs, prudent asset management would seem to dictate some diversification away from the dollar and toward the euro.

Any sizable weakening in the demand for dollar assets by foreign central banks would tend to push down their price and push up U.S. interest rates. This can be expected to have a dampening effect on interest sensitive activities such as business investment, housing, and consumer durables. On the other hand, the selling off of dollar assets would tend to depreciate the dollar's exchange rate and provide a boost to exchange rate sensitive activities of exporting and import-competing industries. From the standpoint of the global economy the efficiency advantages of primarily using dollar reserves may be offset by the enhanced stability of more diversified official holdings.[12]

## End Notes

[1] International Monetary Fund, *Global Financial Stability Report*, World Economic and Financial Surveys, April 2007, pp. 74-76.

[2] U.S. Department of the Treasury, *Treasury Bulletin* (Washington: April 2007), p. 56.

[3] See CRS Report RL32462, *Foreign Investment in U.S. Securities*, by James K. Jackson.

[4] See CRS Report RS21951, *The U.S. Trade Deficit: Role of Foreign Governments*, Marc Labonte and Gail Makinen.

[5] See Mathew Higgens and Thomas Klitgaard, "Reserve Accumulation: Implications for Global Capital Flows," Federal Reserve Bank of New York, *Current Issues in Economics and Finance*, vol. 10, no. 10, October 2004.

[6] Barry Eichengreen, *Sterling's Past, Dollar's Future: Historical Perspectives on Reserve Currency Competition*, National Bureau of Economic Research, Working Paper no. 11336, April 2005.

[7] See B.J. Cohen, *Life at the Top: International Currencies in the 21st Century*, Princeton Essays in International Finance No. 221 (Princeton: December 2000).

[8] A fuller discussion of these four considerations can be found in Barry Eichengreen and Donald Mathieson, *The Currency Composition of Foreign Exchange Reserves – Retrospect and Prospect*, IMF Working Paper no. 00/131, July 2000.

[9] IMF Statistics Department, COFER database.

[10] This discussion in this section closely follows the analysis in a recent BIS study. See Gabriele Galati and Phillip Woodbridge, *The Euro as a Reserve Currency: The Challenge to the Pre-Eminence of the U.S. Dollar*, Bank for International Settlements, BIS Working Papers no. 218, October 2006.

[11] BIS, Central Bank Survey of Foreign Exchange and Derivatives Markets Activity (Basel: March 2005)

[12] Many economists argue that it would be preferable to have one international currency rather than a national currency playing that role. Special Drawing Rights (SDR) is a currency created by the IMF in 1969 as a substitute for the dollar and gold (or any other national currency) as a reserve currency. It has never assumed a major role in international finance, however.

In: Dollar Depreciation
Editor: Lachlan S. Roy

ISBN: 978-1-61470-692-2
© 2011 Nova Science Publishers, Inc.

*Chapter 4*

# THE U.S. TRADE DEFICIT, THE DOLLAR, AND THE PRICE OF OIL[*]

## *James K. Jackson*

## SUMMARY

Rapid changes in the price of oil and the impact of such price changes on economies around the globe have attracted considerable attention. In mid-2008 as the price of oil rose to unprecedented heights and then dropped sharply, the international exchange value of the dollar fell and then rose relative to a broad basket of currencies. For some, these two events seem to indicate a cause and effect relationship between changes in the price of oil and changes in the value of the dollar. Despite common perceptions that there is a direct cause and effect relationship between changes in the international exchange value of the dollar and the price of oil, an analysis of data during recent periods indicates that changes in the price of oil are driven by changes in the demand for oil that is different from the supply of oil, rather than changes in the value of the dollar. The rapid increase in oil prices in early 2011 reflects rising demand for oil and other commodities and uncertainty in global markets keyed to political turmoil in North Africa and the Middle East.

This report analyzes the relationship between the dollar and the price of oil and how the two might interact. While the data do not support a strong cause and effect relationship between the value of the dollar and

---

[*] This is an edited, reformatted and augmented version of a Congressional Research Service publication, CRS Report for Congress RL34686, from www.crs.gov, dated March 2, 2011.

the price of oil, there likely are various channels through which changes in the price of oil and in the value of the dollar may be indirectly correlated. The data also indicate that an increase in the demand for crude oil that exceeded the increase in the supply of oil and a laggardly pace in oil production capacity likely are among the main factors behind the sharp run up in the price of oil that occurred over the first seven months of 2008. The rise in oil prices also affected the U.S. trade deficit. That impact lessened as the price of oil plummeted and as a drop in economic activity reduced demand for oil imports. This report provides an assessment of the impact a range of prices of imported oil could have on the U.S. trade deficit.

## OVERVIEW

To most observers, it seems apparent that the rise in the price of oil[1] and the decline in the exchange value of the dollar often are interconnected events, or that there is some cause and effect relationship between the two.[2] Since oil is priced in dollars, this line of reasoning goes, as the exchange value of the dollar declines, the purchasing power of oil producers also falls, which, in turn, prods oil producers to reduce their supplies to the market in order to push up the market price of oil and restore their purchasing power. This line of thinking is not unreasonable, considering various incidents, most notably 1973 and 1979, in which the price of oil rose sharply in response to actions taken by members of the Organization of Petroleum Exporting Countries (OPEC)[3] group of oil producers to increase the market price of oil. Indeed, OPEC's stated objective is to coordinate and unify petroleum policies among OPEC Countries, in order to secure "fair and stable prices for petroleum producers; an efficient, economic and regular supply of petroleum to consuming nations; and a fair return on capital to those investing in the industry." After reaching nearly $147 per barrel in August 2008, the price per barrel of oil dropped to less than $40 per barrel by year-end 2008, before rising again through February 2011 to reach as high as $120 per barrel at times. In response to the drop in oil prices in 2008, OPEC announced cuts in production on three occasions: a cut of 500,000 barrels per day announced on September 1, 2008,[4] a cut of 1.5 million barrels per day announced on October 25, 2008, and a cut of 2.2 million barrels per day announced on December 17, 2008. In February 2011, Saudi Arabia increased oil production to calm market fears over political unrest in North Africa and the Middle East, particularly concerns over the impact political turmoil on Libya could have on oil production there.

An analysis of the data indicates that the rise and fall in oil prices that has been experienced since 2006 has not been driven primarily by a reduction in world supplies. Instead, the changes in oil prices reflect a number of factors, including the slow-paced growth in oil production; an increase in demand, most notably among the developing countries, that has outpaced the increase in supply; and more recently market concerns related to political turmoil. Changes in the international exchange value of the dollar, however, likely reflect a number of factors, including changes in the demand for and supply of capital within the U.S. economy, the relative rate of return on interest-sensitive assets, and expectations about the performance of the U.S. economy. At the same time, some observers have argued that oil market speculators played an important role in pushing up oil prices so quickly in 2008.[5] A report issued on September 11, 2008, by the Commodity Futures Trading Commission (CFTC), however, concluded that market speculators probably were not responsible for the rise in oil prices.[6]

While data on exchange rates and on oil prices do not support the case for a strong cause and effect relationship between the value of the dollar and the price of oil, there are a number of channels through which changes in the price of oil and changes in the value of the dollar may be indirectly correlated. In fact, an increase in the price of oil to offset the loss of purchasing power that is associated with a depreciation in the value of the dollar can spark a chain of events that could blunt or even nullify the rise in oil prices.

The pervasive nature of such commodities as oil, which serve as essential components in economic growth, means that changes in the prices of those commodities affect the prices of a broad range of goods, services, and economic activities.[7] Indeed, according to the Census Bureau, increases in the price of imported oil were a major factor in rising consumer prices in the United States in the first six months of 2008. Similarly, rising oil prices in late 2010 and early 2011 have pushed up the prices of other commodities. Rising consumer and commodity prices undermine the exchange value of the dollar relative to other currencies and reduce the real incomes of consumers, which can lead to a lower rate of economic growth. Slower economic growth, in turn, lowers the demand for oil, thereby putting downward pressure on the price of oil, as occurred in 2009.[8] Expectations about future economic growth and, therefore, about the demand for crude oil, also can affect a broad range of investment decisions that might affect expectations about the value of the dollar. The interaction between the price of oil and the value of the dollar is complicated further by the way changes in the price of oil can affect the economic performance of other nations and, therefore, have an impact on their respective currencies.[9]

According to Global Insight,[10] a number of factors worked to put upward pressure on oil prices in 2007 and during the first half of 2008. These factors include both supply and demand issues as well as geopolitical troubles in various countries, particularly Nigeria and Iran, that created uncertainties in the market concerning the stability of oil supplies. A low rate of growth in oil supplies relative to a higher rate of growth in the demand for oil has been cited as the most important market factor behind the rise in oil prices. Saudi Arabia agreed to increase its production of oil by 300,000 barrels per day in May 2008 and by an additional 200,000 barrels per day in July 2008. Also, price movements in the oil market apparently were exaggerated somewhat by trading in the oil futures market, and other producers, especially non-OPEC producers, who had not increased their supply as had been projected. On the demand side, continued strong growth in the demand for oil in Asia and the Middle East pushed the total demand for oil to rise at a pace that has been faster than the rise in supplies. Demand in the Middle East rose at double-digit rates as a result of a boom in construction and oil consumption. In Asia, demand for oil grew rapidly in China, where the government subsidized the price of oil to consumers and the government stockpiled oil to use as substitute for coal in the Beijing area during the Olympics to reduce the level of air pollution.

## THE DOLLAR AND THE PRICE OF OIL

For many observers, there seems to be a direct cause and effect relationship between the depreciation in the international exchange value of the dollar and the rise in the price of oil. These observers argue that because oil is priced in dollars, a depreciation in the international exchange value for the dollar against other major currencies erodes the purchasing power of oil producers. The International Monetary Fund (IMF) has identified three channels through which a change in the value of the dollar can affect a broad range of commodity prices, including the price of oil. A change in the value of the dollar can affect commodity prices through (1) purchasing power and cost channels; (2) asset channels in which changes in the value of the dollar affect the return on dollar-denominated financial assets; and (3) a combination of effects, including changes in monetary policy.[11] As a result of these three effects, the IMF also estimates that among various commodities, the linkage between changes in the value of the dollar and changes in commodity prices is especially strong for oil and gold, because they are more suitable as a "store of value," or as a hedge against inflation.[12] One explanation for this relationship is that oil market participants and speculators may have adopted a rough rule of thumb over time concerning changes in the value of the dollar and subsequent changes in the price of oil and vice versa. As a consequence the statistical relationship between the two has been strengthened, because market participants have acted on this informal rule. In late 2010 and early 2011, however, the rise in commodity prices, including the price of oil, appear not to be related to the value of the dollar, since commodity prices rose significantly in terms of all major currencies.

The past actions of OPEC oil producers may also have tended to strengthen the apparent linkage between changes in the value of the dollar and changes in the price of oil as the producers have acted in concert to adjust their output in order to alter the world price of oil. OPEC accounts for just over 40% of the world output of crude oil, and the coordinated actions of its members can affect world oil prices. In addition, one of OPEC's stated goals is to secure a "fair and stable price" for the oil the member countries produce; it is not unreasonable to assume that OPEC members would respond to a loss in the purchasing power of the dollar by reducing their overall level of production, or holding down the rate of increase in production in order to raise the market price of oil.[13]

## Real and Nominal Oil Prices

Figure 1 shows indexes of the nominal and real (adjusted for inflation) indexes of the price of crude oil from 1970 to 2010. The figure shows the 1973 and 1979 price increases and the slide in the real price of oil between 1980 and 1999. The indexes show the stark rise in real oil prices in the 1970s as OPEC oil producers pushed up crude oil prices. Over the next decade, however, real prices slowly moved downward to more moderate levels, due in part to an increase in crude oil production by non-OPEC producers. Naturally, nominal prices increased in the 1970s as a result of the rise in oil prices, but nominal prices rose at a slower pace than real prices as national governments focused economic policies on constraining inflation. Both real and nominal oil prices began rising in 1999 as a result of an agreement signed in 1998 between OPEC members and such non-OPEC producers as Mexico, Norway, Oman, and the Russian Federation to reduce their supplies of oil. While OPEC's production of crude oil declined by about 4% in 1999 from that produced in 1998, production in 2000 increased by 6% to reach an average of 28 million barrels per day. From 2000 to 2002, OPEC's production of crude oil fell by about 9.5% to 25.6 million barrels per day. After 2002, OPEC's crude oil production has increased every year, reaching an average of 33.9 million barrels per day in 2009.

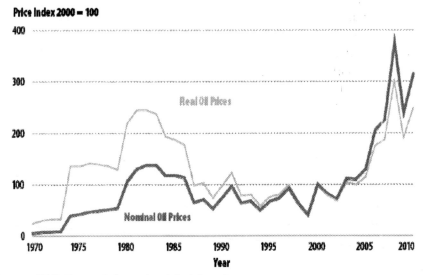

Source: CRS, Energy Information Administration.

Figure 1. Real and Nominal Crude Oil Price Indexes, 1970-2010.

Data for the fourth quarter of 2010 show that the real price of crude oil began rising during the first quarter of 2009 and rose steadily throughout the period, reaching an average price of about two-thirds of that reached during the peak period in 2008. On an annual basis, the average price of oil, as measured by the spot price of Brent crude,[14] rose from an average price of $54.42 per barrel in 2005 to an average of $96.85 per barrel in 2008, or an increase of 78% in nominal terms. During the same period, the dollar depreciated about 10% in real terms as measured against a broad basket of currencies.[15] From January 2008 to July 2008, the real price of oil increased by another 38%, while the real broad dollar index depreciated by 1.7%. Relative to other major currencies, the dollar depreciated about 7% against the Euro in real, or price adjusted terms on average from 2005 to 2008 and about 5.6% in the January to July period in 2008. Relative to the Yen, the average value of the dollar depreciated about 15% between 2005 and 2008 in real terms, and depreciated about 5% against the Yen in the first seven months of 2008. Against the British Pound, the dollar depreciated about 8% in real terms between 2005 and 2008, and fell by about 3% in value in real terms in the first seven months of 2008. From 2009 through 2010, the dollar has appreciated slightly against a broad basket of currencies in real terms and against the pound and the euro, but depreciated against the yen in real terms.

## Major Currencies

Figures 2 through 5 display indexes of the dollar relative to other currencies in real terms and an index of the price of oil, also expressed in real terms, from the first quarter of 1999 through the fourth quarter of 2010. Figure 2 shows the real broad dollar index, or an index of the dollar per a unit of a grouping of 26 currencies in real terms compared with an index of the real price of crude oil. A decline in the dollar index signifies a depreciation in the value of the dollar relative to the broad group of other currencies. The data cast doubt on the argument that the price of oil responded to offset the depreciation of the dollar. Compared with the currencies of the 26 largest U.S. trading partners, the dollar has fluctuated slightly in real terms, compared with large swings in the real price of oil.

Source: Federal Reserve, Energy Information Administration.

Figure 2. Crude Oil Real Price Index and Broad Real Dollar Index,1999-2010.

The devaluation of the dollar against the Euro from early 2006 to the end of 2008 led some observers to speculate that oil producers would attempt to raise the price of oil to compensate for the devalued purchasing power of the dollar relative to the Euro and that a devalued dollar would be a disincentive for producers to explore and drill for new wells because of the loss of purchasing power. In addition, the devalued dollar makes oil cheaper for the Euro-area countries and, therefore, oil consumption in the euro area should increase with an appreciation of the euro. The decline in the exchange value of the dollar relative to the Euro also prompted some observers to argue that oil should be priced in a currency other than the dollar.

Data through fourth quarter 2010, however, do not support the contention that Euro-area countries increased their consumption of oil any faster than the United States due to the drop in the price of oil that resulted from an appreciation of the euro relative to the dollar. Also, after some initial adjustment, pricing oil in Euros, or some other currency, rather than in dollars would appear to have no real effect on the demand and supply of oil in the market. Between the third quarter of 2009 and the third quarter of 2010, as the Euro generally depreciated relative to the dollar, oil consumption of oil in Europe rose by 2.9% compared with an increase in consumption by the United States of 4.1%. Pricing oil in dollars facilitates the smooth functioning of the oil market, because the dollar is the most widely used currency in the world for pricing, or invoicing trade, which facilitates the cross-border comparison of goods and services.[16] Figure 3 shows an index of crude oil prices in real terms and dollars per Euro in real terms, so that a rise in the dollar/Euro index signifies an appreciation in the Euro relative to the dollar, or a depreciation in the value of the dollar. The data support the argument that any loss in oil producers' purchasing power arising from a depreciation in the value of the dollar relative to the Euro was offset by a larger increase in the price of oil, which may well provide an incentive to oil producers to expand their drilling and exploration activities.

Similar trends are seen in movements in the value of the dollar relative to the Yen and the British Pound. Figure 4 shows the index of the Yen per dollar exchange rate, expressed in real terms and the index of the real price of crude oil. In this figure, a decline in the index indicates an appreciation in the value of the Yen relative to the dollar, since fewer Yen are required to buy a dollar. Figure 5 shows the index for dollars per Pounds expressed in real terms and the index for real crude oil prices. In this case, a rise in the dollar/Pound index indicates an appreciation in the value of the Pound, since more dollars would be required to purchase a Pound. In both cases, the relative movement in the real prices of foreign currency against the dollar has been small relative to the increase in the real price of crude oil since 2004.

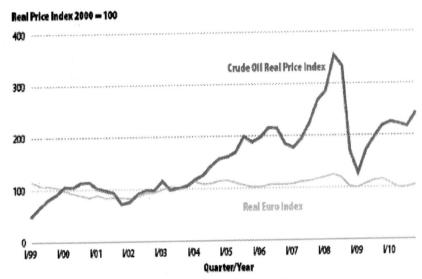

Source: Federal Reserve, Energy Information Administration.

Figure 3. Crude Oil Real Price Index and Real Dollar/Euro Index, 1999-2010.

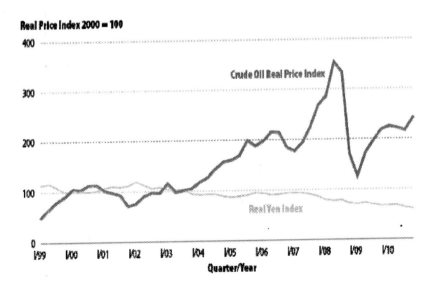

Figure 4. Crude Oil Real Price Index and Real Yen/Dollar Index, 1999-2010.

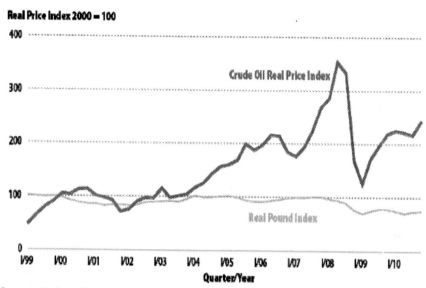

Source: Federal Reserve, Energy Information Administration.

Figure 5. Crude Oil Real Price index and Real Dollar/Pound Index, 1999-2010.

# THE PRICE OF OIL

As indicated previously, the OPEC cartel of oil producers has acted in concert on occasion to alter the supply of oil in the market in order to affect the price of oil and, therefore, the export earnings of its members. In practice, OPEC oil producers, or other oil producers for that matter, do not attempt to set the price of oil directly, but attempt to alter the supply of oil in the market relative to a given level of expected demand and then rely on the market to search out the corresponding price. The price of oil, then, reflects the actual level of demand and supply in the market, which is reflected in the spot, or current, market, and the price of oil is affected by expectations about demand and supply conditions and about production capacity, reflected in the futures market. In addition, during times of economic or political instability, investors may well trade such commodities as oil that they calculate will generate a return on their investment that exceeds such traditional financial investments as stocks, bonds, or government securities.

## Oil Exchanges

Similar to other commodities, oil is traded on specialized commodities exchanges. Most of this trading is conducted by licensed brokers, who act on behalf of clients to buy and sell oil on the spot market and in the futures and options markets.[17] The major futures exchanges for oil are the Intercontinental Exchange, located in London, which acquired the International Petroleum Exchange in 2001, and the New York Mercantile Exchange (NYMEX). The New York Exchange states that it is the world's largest physical commodity futures exchange. The NYMEX operates on the bid-ask system in which buy and sell transactions are executed between floor brokers. In this process, buyers compete with each other by bidding up prices and sellers compete by bidding prices down. Such markets are identified as price discovery markets, because the price of the futures contract is determined through open bids. Futures contracts are firm commitments to make or accept delivery of a specified quantity and quality of a commodity during a specified month in the future at a price agreed upon at the time the contract is made. In the commodities exchanges, futures contracts are traded in standardized units in a highly visible, extremely competitive continuous open auction. The NYMEX reports that less than 1% of all oil futures contracts take physical delivery; the remainder are settled by cash payments.

Although relatively little physical quantities of oil change hands in futures markets, the markets serve as important sources of information about market conditions and provide mechanisms for determining the price of oil in the global energy market. As a result, oil prices that are determined in the futures market are useful in at least three ways.[18] First, since the futures markets are conducted in full public view, a broad assortment of traders, including producers, commercial users, speculators, and financial institutions, make financial and production decisions based on the prices that are determined in the market. Second, the prices that are generated in the futures markets are publicly available and are used as reference points for physical trades in oil. Third, because the markets are conducted on a bid-ask system with floor brokers, the prices react quickly to new information about the supply and demand factors that are expected to influence the price of oil.

Futures and options contacts are used by both buyers and sellers to reduce the risks inherent in trading commodities.[19] Factors that might cause an abrupt change in supply, demand, and price such as international politics, war, changing economic patterns, and structural changes within the energy industry have created uncertainty about market conditions. Such uncertainty, in turn, leads to volatility in the market and creates risk for the market participants. The futures price, then, represents the current market opinion of what the commodity will be worth at some time in the future. Since the future price of a commodity can not be known with any certainty, buyers and sellers attempt to lock in prices and profit margins in advance through the use of futures and options contracts in order to hedge, or to reduce, their risks. The purpose of the hedge is to avoid the risk of an abrupt change in market conditions and prices that could result in major losses for buyers and sellers.

Since the spot price and the futures market price do not have a perfect relationship, there will always be the potential for some profit or loss. Hedging, then, reduces exposure to risk for a buyer or a seller by shifting part of the risk associated with the market price of a commodity to investors who are willing to accept the risk in exchange for a profit opportunity. As indicated above, most traders do not take physical delivery of the commodities they are trading, but hope to profit by correctly anticipating future price trends, which some observers argue has been a factor in driving high and volatile prices. Concerns over the impact of such trading on the oil market spurred a number of legislative proposals during the 110th Congress.[20]

Unlike a futures contract, an options contract conveys a right, but not an obligation, to engage in a transaction. There are two types of options, calls and puts. A call conveys the right, but not the obligation, to the one holding the option to purchase the underlying futures contract at a specified price up to a certain time. A put gives the owner of the option the right, but not the obligation, to sell the underlying futures contract at a specified price up to a certain time. A call is purchased when investors anticipate a rise in prices and a put is bought when investors expect neutral or falling prices. When options are used in combination with futures contracts, investors can develop strategies that cover virtually any risk profile, time horizon, or cost consideration.

## Oil Demand and Supply

The data in Table 1 show the world demand and supply of petroleum in millions of barrels a day on average by major area from 2004 through 2009, including the first three quarters of 2010. As indicated in Figure 6, between 2005 and 2009, the demand for oil, or consumption, among all consumers increased by 0.8%, rising from an average of 83.65 million barrels per day in 2005 to an average of 84.33 million barrels per day in 2009. Data for 2009 indicate that world demand for oil fell below the average for 2008 as economic growth slowed as a consequence of the financial crisis and the global economic recession. Over the first three quarters of 2010, however, world demand for oil increased by 2.4%, with demand among the developed economies increasing by 1.6% and demand increasing by 3.4% among the developing economies. The developed economies, represented by the members of the Organization for Economic Cooperation and Development (OECD),[21] accounted for about 60% of world demand for oil. As a group, these developed economies decreased their demand for oil every year between 2005 and 2008. Oil demand fell in most countries and areas in 2008 as the pace of global economic activity slowed from the faster pace in 2007. On average, oil demand among OECD countries fell by 3.6% between 2007 and 2008, compared with a 3.6% increase in demand among non-OECD countries over the same period. During the 2005-2009 period, demand for oil by the developed OECD countries fell by 7.9% and by 9.8% in the United States. Among the developing countries, oil demand between 2005 and 2009 increased by 13.6%, led by a 23.9% increase in demand by China, although such demand started from a low base.

During the 2005-2009 period, oil supplies fell by 3.6% among the developed countries, or falling by about half as much as the demand for oil among the developed countries, effectively increasing their demand for oil on world markets. During the same five-year period, oil supplies among the developing countries increased by 0.9%, led by an increase in supplies by developing countries other than OPEC countries and Russia.

Figure 7 shows that world oil supplies fell by 2.8% over the period from 2005 to 2009, or by less than the increase in the world demand for oil. During this period, oil supplies provided by U.S. producers increased by nearly 10%, while oil production in other developed countries fell by 3.9%. At the same time, OPEC producers decreased their supply of oil by 6.2%, mostly during the 2008-2009 period, and oil suppliers from other developing countries increased their supplies by 0.9%. The shortfall between the change in demand and the change in supply was met by oil that had been held in stocks elsewhere. The rising demand likely was an important factor in pushing up the price of oil in the market and likely affected the pricing expectations of oil brokers and traders in the futures market.

**Table 1. World Oil Demand and Supply, 2005-2010 (million barrels per day)**

|  | 2005 | 2006 | 2007 | 2008 | 2009 | 2010 | | | |
|---|---|---|---|---|---|---|---|---|---|
|  | Annual Average | | | | | Quarter | | | |
|  |  |  |  |  |  | 1st | 2nd | 3rd | 4th |
| **Petroleum (Oil) Demand** | | | | | | | | | |
| OECD | | | | | | | | | |
| United States | 20.80 | 20.69 | 20.68 | 19.50 | 18.77 | 18.82 | 19.01 | 19.49 | NA |
| Other OECD | 15.61 | 15.63 | 28.44 | 28.05 | 26.95 | 27.21 | 26.44 | 27.29 | |
| Total OECD | 49.66 | 49.34 | 49.59 | 47.87 | 45.72 | 46.03 | 45.45 | 46.78 | |
| Non-OECD | | | | | | | | | |
| China | 6.72 | 7.20 | 7.58 | 7.83 | 8.32 | 8.88 | 9.31 | 8.89 | |
| Former U.S.S.R. | 4.07 | 4.21 | 4.27 | 4.35 | 4.21 | 4.31 | 4.33 | 4.48 | |
| Other Non-OECD | 23.20 | 23.88 | 24.84 | 25.72 | 26.08 | 26.20 | 27.27 | 27.35 | |
| Total Non-OECD | 33.99 | 35.29 | 36.70 | 37.90 | 38.6 | 39.39 | 40.91 | 40.72 | |
| Total World Demand | 83.65 | 84.62 | 86.29 | 85.78 | 84.33 | 85.42 | 86.36 | 87.50 | |
| **Petroleum (Oil) Supply** | | | | | | | | | |
| OECD | | | | | | | | | |
| United States | 8.32 | 8.33 | 8.46 | 8.51 | 9.14 | 9.45 | 9.56 | 9.67 | |
| Other OECD | 13.56 | 13.26 | 13.03 | 12.43 | 11.95 | 11.93 | 11.55 | 11.20 | |
| Total OECD | 21.88 | 21.59 | 21.48 | 20.95 | 21.09 | 21.38 | 21.11 | 20.87 | |

|  | 2005 | 2006 | 2007 | 2008 | 2009 | 2010 | | | |
|  | Annual Average | | | | | Quarter | | | |
|  |  |  |  |  |  | 1st | 2nd | 3rd | 4th |
| Non-OECD |  |  |  |  |  |  |  |  |  |
| OPEC | 36.09 | 35.83 | 34.39 | 35.71 | 33.87 | 34.45 | 34.65 | 34.84 |  |
| Former U.S.S.R. | 11.77 | 12.16 | 12.61 | 12.53 | 12.91 | 13.12 | 13.16 | 13.20 |  |
| Other Non-OECD | 14.89 | 15.02 | 16.07 | 16.32 | 16.52 | 16.96 | 17.09 | 17.19 |  |
| Total Non-OECD | 62.75 | 63.01 | 63.06 | 64.56 | 63.30 | 64.53 | 64.90 | 65.23 |  |
| Total World Supply | 84.63 | 84.60 | 84.54 | 85.51 | 84.39 | 85.90 | 86.02 | 86.10 |  |
| Difference (demand less supply) | -0.98 | 0.02 | 1.75 | 0.27 | -0.05 | -0.48 | 0.34 | 1.40 |  |

Source: *International Petroleum Monthly*, December, 2010. Energy Information Administration. Table 2.1.

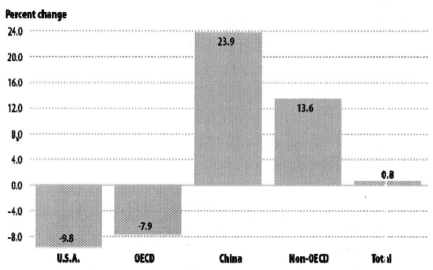

Source: Energy Information Administration.

Figure 6. Change in Oil Demand by Major Area, 2005 to 2009.

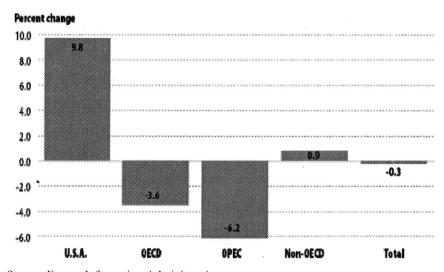

Source: Energy Information Administration.

Figure 7. Change in Oil Supply by Major Area, 2005 to 2009.

# THE INTERNATIONAL EXCHANGE VALUE OF THE DOLLAR

Although attention has focused on the international exchange value of the dollar for many years, the general depreciation of the dollar since 2006 has drawn particular attention. As previously stated, some observers have argued that the rise in the price of oil has occurred in part to offset the decline in the purchasing power of oil producers as a result of the depreciation of the dollar against other major currencies. According to standard economic theory, the international exchange value of the dollar is determined by a complex interplay of demand for and supply of goods and capital within the U.S. economy and the demand for and supply of dollars in international currency markets. While dollar-related transactions generally are independent of those transactions that determine the market price of oil, there may be channels through which movements in the price of oil and changes in the value of the dollar may have spillover effects. This is especially true for the price of oil, which has a far-ranging impact on the performance of the U.S. economy and on global flows of dollars. Over time, such a connection may have become more stylized in the minds of some observers who may link changes in the price of oil to changes in the value of the dollar and vice versa. Such global capital flows, in turn, are facilitated by liberalized international capital markets and floating exchange rates, which greatly expand the amount of capital flows between countries. These flows also have sparked growth in the development and the use of financial instruments that are designed to ease the international trade of currencies and to provide investors, corporations, and financial services providers with a hedge against unpredictable changes in the value of currencies.

## Capital Flows

Capital inflows also help bridge the gap in the United States between the amount of credit demanded and the domestic supply of funds. A shortfall in the domestic supply of credit relative to domestic demands for those funds tends to raise domestic interest rates and draws in capital from abroad. Those inflows, in turn, help to keep U.S. interest rates below the level they likely would reach without the inflows. The necessity to attract capital inflows, however, has complicated the conduct of economic policy. As the Federal Reserve has lowered interest rates on credit in order to stimulate economic activity and stem a slowdown in the economy, the lower interest rates have blunted capital inflows as foreign investors have sought assets in other markets where relative interest rates are higher.

Capital inflows, however, do allow the United States to spend beyond its means, including financing its trade deficit, because foreigners have been willing to lend to the United States in the form of exchanging goods, represented by U.S. imports, for such U.S. assets as stocks, bonds, and U.S. Treasury securities. Such inflows put upward pressure on the dollar, because demand for U.S. assets, such as financial securities, translates into demand for the dollar, since U.S. securities are denominated in dollars. As demand for the dollar rises or falls according to overall demand for dollar-denominated assets, the value of the dollar changes. These exchange rate changes, in turn, have secondary effects on the prices of U.S. and foreign goods, which tend to alter the U.S. trade balance. In addition, an increase in the U.S. rate of inflation tends to undermine the value of the dollar relative to other currencies, which tends to shift demand from the dollar to other currencies. At times, foreign governments have intervened in international capital markets to acquire the dollar directly or to acquire Treasury securities in order to strengthen the value of the dollar against particular currencies.

### U.S. Financial Balance

The most common way of measuring capital inflows is through the U.S. balance of payments accounts. According to standard economic theory, macroeconomic developments in the U.S. economy are the major driving forces behind the magnitudes of capital flows, because the macroeconomic factors determine the overall demand for and supply of credit in the economy. Naturally, these macroeconomic conditions can be affected by changes in the price of oil, or by changes in macroeconomic policies. To the extent that changes in the price of oil alter the basic savings-investment relationship in the economy, such price changes could have long-lasting impact on the economy and on the trade balance.

One way of viewing the interaction between capital inflows and the domestic demand and supply of funds is through the domestic flow of funds accounts. These accounts measure financial flows across sectors of the economy, tracking funds as they move from those sectors that supply the capital through intermediaries to sectors that use the capital to acquire physical and financial assets.[22] Table 2 shows the major accounts in the net flow of funds in the U.S. economy from 1996 through the third quarter of 2010 The net flows show the overall financial position by sector, whether that sector is a net supplier or a net user of financial capital in the economy. Since the demand for funds in the economy as a whole must equal the supply of funds, a deficit in one sector must be offset by a surplus in another sector.

### Table 2. Flow of Funds of the U.S. Economy, 1996-2010
### (billions of dollars)

| Year | Households | Businesses | Total | State and Local | Federal | ROW |
|------|-----------|-----------|-------|----------------|---------|-----|
|  |  |  | Government | | | |
| 1996 | 175.2 | 19.8 | -196.8 | -1.2 | -195.6 | 137.9 |
| 1997 | 47.4 | -18.3 | -116.6 | -47.5 | -69.1 | 219.6 |
| 1998 | 128.0 | -45.7 | 64.8 | 48.8 | 16.0 | 75.0 |
| 1999 | -132.7 | -62.6 | 115.3 | 9.9 | 105.4 | 231.7 |
| 2000 | -371.0 | -82.9 | 252.5 | 54.5 | 198.0 | 476.3 |
| 2001 | -494.4 | -82.9 | 233.4 | 35.4 | 198.0 | 485.4 |
| 2002 | -304.0 | 8.7 | -382.6 | -95.6 | -287.0 | 501.7 |
| 2003 | -79.3 | 30.3 | -546.3 | -70.4 | -476.4 | 529.4 |
| 2004 | -67.9 | 136.8 | -468.1 | -33.0 | -436.1 | 530.0 |
| 2005 | -466.5 | -44.8 | -373.1 | 7.3 | -380.4 | 712.1 |
| 2006 | -512.2 | -231.1 | -188.9 | 76.1 | -265.0 | 807.4 |
| 2007 | 70.5 | -285.1 | -345.0 | -1.7 | -343.3 | 638.5 |
| 2008 | 619.1 | -1,003.1 | -914.9 | -137.3 | -777.6 | 583.9 |
| 2009 | 273.8 | 211.9 | -1,399.9 | -85.1 | -1,314.8 | 215.9 |
| 2010 I | 392.5 | 262.0 | -1,445.1 | -39.5 | -1,405.6 | 138.7 |
| 2010 II | 1,091.0 | 12.6 | -1,814.9 | -48.4 | -1,766.5 | 146.3 |
| 2010 III | 252.7 | 181.9 | -1,079.3 | 14.8 | -1,094.1 | 259.4 |

Source: Board of Governors of the Federal Reserve System, Flow of Funds Accounts of the United States, Flows and Outstandings Third Quarter 2010, December 9, 2010.

Note: Negative values indicate a net inflow of funds, or that the demand for funds in that sector was greater than the supply of funds provided by that sector.

Generally, the household sector, or individuals, provides funds to the economy, because individuals save part of their income, while the business sector uses those funds to invest in plant and equipment that, in turn, serve as the building blocks for the production of additional goods and services. The government sector (the combination of federal, state, and local governments) can be either a net supplier of funds or a net user, depending on whether the sector is running a surplus or a deficit, respectively. The interplay within the economy between saving and investment, or the supply and uses of funds, tends to affect domestic interest rates, which move to equate the demand and supply of funds. Shifts in the interest rate also tend to attract capital from abroad, denoted by the rest of the world (ROW).

From 1999 until late in 2006, the household sector was dissaving, as individuals spent more than they earned. Part of this dissaving was offset by the government sector, which experienced a surplus from 1998 to 2001. As a result of the large household dissaving, however, the economy as a whole experienced a gap between domestic saving and .investment that was filled with large capital inflows. Those inflows were particularly large in nominal terms from 2000 to 2008, as household dissaving continued and as government sector surpluses turned to historically large deficits in nominal terms. Such inflows kept interest rates below the level they would have reached without the inflows, but they put added pressure on the international exchange value of the dollar during that period.

In 2008 and 2009, capital inflows fell sharply, reflecting the global financial crisis and economic recession and the associated drop in international trade. This drop in capital inflows reflected a shift by households from dissaving to saving as concerns over the economy, with an attendant large loss in personal wealth, spurred households to pare back their consumption expenditures and to increase their personal savings. The business sector also shifted from a net supplier of funds in 2007 to a net consumer of funds as investments declined, again reflecting tight credit conditions and the drop in the rate of economic growth in the economy in 2008 and 2009. Both the federal government and state and local governments experienced a deterioration in their accounts as these sectors of the economy experienced large net deficits, reflecting the slowing rate of growth in the U.S. economy. The decrease in capital inflows combined with the slowing rate of economic growth and concerns about the stability of the financial services sector likely placed downward pressure on the exchange value of the dollar, or a devalue-ation of the dollar.

## Foreign Exchange Market

International factors also affect the value of the dollar. The dollar is heavily traded in financial markets around the globe and, at times, plays the role of a global currency. Disruptions in this role have important implications for the United States and for the smooth functioning of the international financial system. This prominent role means that the exchange value of the dollar often acts as a mechanism for transmitting economic and political news and events across national borders, including expectations about the performance of the economy and concerns about the impact of such supply factors as the rise in the price of oil. While such a role helps facilitate a broad range of international economic and financial activities, it also means that the dollar's exchange value can vary greatly on a daily or weekly basis as it is buffeted by international events.

**Table 3. Foreign Exchange Market Turnover**
**(Daily averages in April of the year indicated, billions of U.S. dollars)**

|  | 1995 | 1998 | 2001 | 2004 | 2007 | 2010 |
|---|---|---|---|---|---|---|
| **Foreign Exchange Market Turnover** | | | | | | |
| Instrument | | | | | | |
| Spot transactions | 494 | 568 | 386 | 631 | 1,005 | 1,490 |
| Outright forwards | 97 | 128 | 130 | 209 | 362 | 475 |
| Foreign exchange swaps | 546 | 734 | 656 | 954 | 1,714 | 1,765 |
| Reporting gaps | 53 | 61 | 28 | 107 | 129 | NA |
| Total "traditional" turnover | 1,190 | 1,527 | 1,239 | 1,934 | 3,324 | 3,981 |
| **Over the Counter Derivatives Market Turnover** | | | | | | |
| Foreign exchange instruments | | 97 | 87 | 140 | 291 | NA |
| Interest rate instruments | | 265 | 489 | 1,025 | 1,686 | 2,083 |
| Reporting gaps | | 13 | 19 | 55 | 113 | NA |
| Total OTC turnover | | 375 | 575 | 1,220 | 1,990 | 2,083 |
| **Total market turnover** | 1,190 | 1,865 | 1,775 | 3,100 | 5,300 | 6,064 |
| **United States** | | | | | | |
| Foreign exchange turnover | 244 | 351 | 254 | 461 | 664 | 817 |
| OTC derivatives turnover | | 90 | 135 | 355 | 607 | 659 |
| Total | 244 | 441 | 389 | 816 | 1,271 | 1,506 |

Source: Triennial Central Bank Survey: Foreign Exchange and Derivatives Market Activity in 2010. Bank for International Settlement, September 2010.

A triennial survey of the world's leading central banks conducted by the Bank for International Settlements in April 2010 indicates that the *daily* trading of foreign currencies through traditional foreign exchange markets[23] totals about $4 trillion, up from the $3.3 trillion reported in the previous survey conducted in 2007, as indicated in Table 3. In addition to the traditional foreign exchange market, the over-the-counter (OTC)[24] foreign exchange derivatives market reported that daily turnover of interest rate and non-traditional foreign exchange derivatives contracts reached $2.1 trillion in April 2010 The combined amount of $6.1 trillion for daily foreign exchange trading in the traditional and OTC markets is more than three times the *annual* amount of U.S. exports of goods and services. The data also indicate that 85% of the global foreign exchange turnover is in U.S. dollars, slightly lower than the 85.6% share reported in a similar survey conducted in 2007.[25]

## The U.S. Trade Deficit

Rising oil prices add to the Nation's trade deficit and boost the rate of change in wholesale and consumer prices, as long as the oil price increases are not offset by actions by the Federal Reserve to tighten the money supply.[26] According to data published by the Census Bureau of the Department of Commerce,[27] the prices of petroleum products over the past year have varied considerably, at times rising faster than the change in demand for those products. As a result, the price increases of imported energy-related petroleum products worsened the U.S. trade deficit in 2006,- 2008 and again in 2010. This rising cost of oil added an estimated $120 billion in 2008 and $80 billion in 2010.[28]

Changes in oil prices also affect the cost of a broad range of goods, services, and economic activities and the changes can affect the real discretionary incomes of consumers, which has an impact on the rate of economic growth. A lower rate of economic growth, as was experienced in late 2008 and in 2009, reduces demand for oil and the price of oil falls to equate supply and demand, assuming that the supply of oil remains constant. The trade deficit also represents a transfer of wealth from the United States to the oil producers. This transfer of wealth reduces the real discretionary incomes of U.S. consumers. To the extent that the additional accumulation of wealth abroad is returned to the United States as payments for additional U.S. exports or to acquire such assets as securities or U.S. businesses, some of the negative effects could be mitigated. The data in Table 4 provide estimates of the impact different prices for imported crude oil could have on the annual U.S. trade deficit. The table also provides estimates for the increase in the trade deficit if the amount, or the volume, of imported oil declined by 3% or rose by 3% on an annual basis, as a result of changes in the demand for oil.

**Table 4. Estimates of the Impact on the U.S. Trade Deficit Associated With Various Prices for Crude Oil and Changes in Oil Import Volumes**

| | 2010 | | 2011 | | | |
|---|---|---|---|---|---|---|
| | (Actual values) | | Estimated values | | | |
| | Quantity (billions of barrels) | Value (billions of dollars) | Price per barrel | | | |
| Price per barrel | | $74.66 | $70.00 | $80.00 | $90.00 | $100.00 |
| Crude oil imports | 3.38 | $252.18 | $236.44 | $270.22 | $303.99 | $337.77 |
| Total energy-related Petroleum | 4.28 | $323.63 | $299.49 | $342.28 | $385.06 | $427.85 |
| Products imports | | | | | | |
| Change in trade deficit (in $billions) | | | $-24.16 | $18.65 | $61.43 | $104.22 |
| **With 3 percent reduction in import volumes** | | | | | | |
| Crude oil imports | | | $229.35 | $262.11 | $294.87 | $327.64 |
| Total energy-related Petroleum Products | | | $290.51 | $332.01 | $373.51 | $415.01 |
| Change in trade deficit (in $billions) | | | $-33.12 | $8.38 | $49.88 | $91.38 |
| **With 3 percent increase in import volumes** | | | | | | |
| Crude oil imports | | | $243.53 | $278.32 | $313.11 | $347.90 |
| Total energy-related Petroleum Products | | | $308.48 | $352.55 | $396.61 | $440.68 |
| Change in trade deficit (in $billions) | | | $-15.15 | $28.92 | $72.98 | $117.05 |

Source: U.S. International Trade in Goods and Services February 2011, Census Bureau. Estimates developed by CRS.

According to the Census Bureau, the United States imported 4.28 billion barrels of energy-related petroleum products in 2010. Energy-related petroleum products is a term used by the Census Bureau that includes crude oil, petroleum preparations, and liquefied propane and butane gas. Crude oil comprises the largest share by far within this broad category of energy-related imports. At an average price of $74.66 per barrel, imported petroleum products cost $323 billion dollars in 2010. After subtracting U.S. exports of petroleum products, the U.S. trade deficit in petroleum products was $265 billion, or 41% of the total trade deficit in 2010 of $646 billion. At an average price of $80 per barrel in 2011 and assuming that the amount, or the volume, of petroleum products the United States imports does not change, the U.S. trade deficit in oil in 2011 would increase by $18 billion over the deficit recorded in 2010. At an average price of $100 per barrel in 2011, the cost of imported petroleum would add $104 billion to the annual trade deficit.

Naturally, should import volumes decrease as a result of greater energy conservation or a lower rate of economic growth, the addition to the annual trade deficit would be less. If import volumes fell by 3% at a time when the average price of imported petroleum products was $100 per barrel, the addition to the annual trade deficit would be $91 billion. Should import volumes increase by 3% and oil prices rise, the deficit would increase as well.

## CONCLUSIONS

Despite common perceptions that there is a direct cause and effect relationship between changes in the international exchange value of the dollar and the price of oil, an analysis of recent data indicates that the rise in the price of oil is being driven by an increase in demand that is exceeding the increase in supply and by political turmoil in North Africa and the Middle East. Attempts by oil producers to raise the market price of oil in order to offset the loss of purchasing power of a depreciating dollar likely would find those efforts blunted partially or in whole by the repercussions of the rise in oil prices. Increases in oil prices tend to push up prices among a broad range of goods, services, and economic activities due to the ubiquitous presence of oil as a source of energy. In addition, higher relative rates of inflation tend to undermine the exchange value of the dollar relative to other currencies, devaluing the dollar relative to other currencies and reducing the purchasing power of the dollar. Domestically, rising commodity prices reduce real incomes and lower the overall level of consumption. In turn, lower consumption reduces economic growth, which would tend to reduce the demand for oil and lead ultimately to a lower market price for oil.

The relationship between the dollar and the price of oil is complicated by the impact the price of oil can have on the rate of inflation and the rate of economic growth in the United States, the rate of economic growth and the rate of inflation in other countries, and effects on foreign currencies. For instance, rising oil prices not only raise the price of energy in the United States, but in countries around the globe. Rising prices, in turn, tend to undermine the purchasing power of national currencies. Depending on the level of domestic dependency on foreign oil, the impact of changes in oil prices can vary. Concerns over rising prices in Europe and the prospect of slowing economic growth in the Euro zone countries have tended to push down the exchange value of the Euro relative to the dollar.[29]

Upward pressure on the market price of crude oil also can come from market participants and investors who are bidding up the price of oil in an effort to invest in commodities that they calculate will generate a rate of return that exceeds that of traditional financial investments. With demand for crude oil rising faster than supplies, it is difficult for the market to determine what the future price of crude oil might be, which provides a climate that is susceptible to speculation, although there is no clear evidence that such speculation has been a major factor in the rise in crude oil prices since 2006.

Over the long run, a sustained increase in the price of energy imports could permanently alter the composition of the nation's merchandise trade deficit. Some of the impact of higher oil prices, however, could be offset if some of the dollars are returned to the U.S. economy through increased purchases of U.S. goods and services or through purchases of such other assets as securities of U.S. businesses. Some of the return in dollars likely will come through sovereign wealth funds (SWFs), or funds controlled and managed by foreign governments, as foreign exchange reserves boost the dollar holdings of such funds. Such investments likely will add to concerns about the national security implications of foreign acquisitions of U.S. firms, especially by foreign governments, and to concerns about the growing share of outstanding U.S. Treasury securities that are owned by foreigners. Over the long run it is possible for the economy to adjust to the higher prices of energy imports by improving its energy efficiency, finding alternative sources of energy, or searching out additional supplies of energy. Increased pressure is already being applied to Congress to assist in this process.

The sharp rise in prices of energy imports experienced since mid-2010 is increasing the U.S. rate of inflation and could have a slightly negative impact on the rate of economic growth in 2011. This could pose a number of policy issues for Congress. A slowdown in the rate of economic growth in the United

States will lessen the demand for energy imports and could help restrain the prices of energy imports, but likely put additional pressure on the budgets at the state, local, and federal levels of government. An important factor will be the length of political turmoil in North Africa and the Middle East and the potential impact Atlantic hurricanes have on the production of crude oil in the Gulf of Mexico. Most immediately, higher prices for energy imports will worsen the nation's merchandise trade deficit, add to inflationary pressures, and have a disproportionate impact on the energy-intensive sectors of the economy and on households on fixed incomes.

For Congress, the increase in the nation's merchandise trade deficit could add to existing inflationary pressures and complicate efforts to stimulate the economy should the rate of economic growth slow down. In particular, Congress, through its direct role in making economic policy and its oversight role over the Federal Reserve, could face the dilemma of rising inflation, which generally is treated by raising interest rates to tighten credit, and a slowing rate of economic growth, which is usually addressed by lowering interest rates to stimulate investment. A sharp rise in the trade deficit could also add to pressures for Congress to examine the causes of the deficit and to address the underlying factors that are generating that deficit. In addition, the rise in prices of energy imports could add to concerns about the nation's reliance on foreign supplies for energy imports and capital inflows and add impetus to examining the nation's energy strategy.

# End Notes

[1] CRS Report RL33521, Gasoline Prices: Causes of Volatility and Congressional Response, by Carl E. Behrens and Carol Glover.
[2] Merriman, Jane, "Weak Dollar Central to Oil Price Boom," Reuters, September 26, 2007.
[3] OPEC is comprised of Algeria, Angola, Ecuador, Indonesia, Iran, Iraq, Kuwait, Libya, Nigeria, Qatar, Saudi Arabia, UAE, and Venezuela.
[4] Reed, Stanley, "How Real is OPEC's Production Cut?" BusinessWeek, September 11, 2008.
[5] Masters, Michael W., Testimony before the Committee on Homeland Security and Governmental affairs, United States Senate, May 20, 2008.
[6] Mufson, Steven, "Speculators Did Not Raise Oil Prices, Regulator Says," The Washington Post, September 12, 2008, p. D1; Staff Report on Commodity Swap Dealers & Index Traders With Commission Recommendations, Commodity Futures Trading Commission, September 2008.
[7] CRS Report RL31608, The Effects of Oil Shocks on the Economy: A Review of the Empirical Evidence, by Marc Labonte.

[8] Clifford, Catherine, Oil at 5-month Low on Shrinking Demand. CNNMoney.com., September 5, 2008; Barr, Colin, Why Cheaper Oil Signals Trouble. CNNMoney.com. September 4, 2008.

[9] Dougherty, Carter, "Fears of European Slowdown Weaken the Euro." The New York Times, August 9, 2008.

[10] Market Analysis: Forecast Highlights, Global Insight, July 1, 2008.

[11] World Economic Outlook, the International Monetary Fund, April 2008. P. 46-50.

[12] The IMF estimates that a 1 percent real depreciation in the value of the dollar would result in an increase of greater than 1 percent in the price of oil over two years. Ibid., p. 50.

[13] According to standard economic theory, a reduction in the market supply of a good relative to a given level of demand will result in a higher market price for the good since the market demand would be chasing a smaller number of goods (supply), which would tend to bid up the market price of the good.

[14] Brent crude is the largest classification of crude oil. It is used to price two-thirds of internationally traded crude oil supplies.

[15] The broad dollar index is an index of the currencies of 26 largest U.S. trading partners weighted by the importance of the country as a trading partner. For additional information, see Loretan, Mico, Indexes of the Foreign Exchange Value of the Dollar, Federal Reserve Bulletin, Winter 2005. P. 1-8.

[16] Goldberg, Linda S., and Cedric Tille, The International Role of the Dollar and Trade Balance Adjustment, NBER Working Paper 12495, August 2006; and Goldberg, Linda S, and Cedric Tille, Macroeconomic Interdependence and the International Role of the Dollar, NBER Working Paper 13820, February 2008.

[17] For additional information, see CRS Report RL34555, Speculation and Energy Prices: Legislative Responses, by Mark Jickling and Lynn J. Cunningham.

[18] CRS Report RS22918, Primer on Energy Derivatives and Their Regulation, by Mark Jickling.

[19] A Guide to Energy Hedging. New York Mercantile Exchange.

[20] Ibid.

[21] For additional information about the OECD, see CRS Report RS21129, Pharmaceutical Patent Term Extensions: A Brief Explanation, by Wendy H. Schacht and John R. Thomas.

[22] Teplin, Albert M., The U.S. Flows of Funds Accounts and Their Uses, Federal Reserve Bulletin, July 2001, pp. 431-441.

[23] Traditional foreign exchange markets are organized exchanges which trade primarily in foreign exchange futures and options contracts where the terms and condition of the contracts are standardized.

[24] The over-the-counter foreign exchange derivatives market is an informal market consisting of dealers who custom-tailor agreements to meet the specific needs regarding maturity, payments intervals or other terms that allow the contracts to meet specific requirements for risk.

[25] Triennial Central Bank Survey: Foreign Exchange and Derivatives Market Activity in 2010. Bank for International Settlement, September 2010. pp. 1-2. A copy of the report is available at http://www.bis.org/publ/rpfx07.pdf

[26] Consumer Price Index: January 2011, The Bureau of Labor Statistics. P. 1.

[27] Census Bureau, Department of Commerce. Report FT900, U.S. International Trade in Goods and Services, February 11, 2011. Table 17. The report and supporting tables are available at http://www.census.gov/foreign-trade/PressRelease/currentjress_release/ftdpress.pdf.

[28] For additional information, see CRS Report RS22204, U.S. Trade Deficit and the Impact of Changing Oil Prices, by James K. Jackson.

[29] Dougherty, Fears of European Slowdown Weaken the Euro.

# CHAPTER SOURCES

Chapter 1 - This is an edited, reformatted and augmented version of a Congressional Research Service publication, RL34582, dated April 15, 2011.

Chapter 2 - This is an edited, reformatted and augmented version of a Congressional Research Service publication, RL34311, dated May 6, 2008.

Chapter 3 - This is an edited, reformatted and augmented version of a Congressional Research Service publication, RL34083, dated July 10, 2007.

Chapter 4 - This is an edited, reformatted and augmented version of a Congressional Research Service publication, RL34686, dated March 2, 2011.

# INDEX

**S**

**T**

**U**